Hiker's Guide to Mount Diablo State Park

Mount Diablo Interpretive Association

MOUNT DIABLO INTERPRETIVE ASSOCIATION

Hiker's Guide to Mount Diablo State Park

Edited by Ruth Ann Kishi
Published by Mount Diablo Interpretive Association

Library of Congress Catalog Card Number: 2015947539
ISBN 978-0-9748925-9-7

Copyrighted photograph on page 130 provided courtesy of Stephen Joseph, Stephen Joseph Fine Art Photography, www.stephenjosephphoto.com

Cover photo by Dereck Love

Designed by Rita Ter Sarkissoff • www.springhillbooks.com
Printed in Korea by AsianPrinting.com

Contents

Introduction

▨ North

▨ South

Interior

West

East

Introduction

California, with its beautiful seashores, magnificent redwoods, fascinating deserts, and numerous other natural wonders, is also home to many urban dwellers. Those of us lucky enough to live in the San Francisco Bay Area have a natural wonder right in our back yard. Mount Diablo is closely surrounded by a dense population of people and freeways, yet it still maintains its unspoiled wilderness. To fully enjoy that wilderness, one only has to step into the park and start walking. This guide is intended to aid visitors interested in exploring by foot the many facets and beauty of 162 miles of hiking trails throughout almost 20,000 acres of Mount Diablo State Park.

This publication was developed by a dedicated group of volunteers whose love of the mountain is revealed in their vivid, descriptive narratives. These volunteers are members of Mount Diablo Interpretive Association (MDIA). MDIA is a non-profit volunteer organization that assists the California Department of Parks and Recreation in maintaining and interpreting Mount Diablo State Park for its hundreds of thousands of visitors each year. Through a continuing program of education, sponsored activities and publications, MDIA fosters appreciation and the enlightened use of Mount Diablo State Park.

✳ THE PARK'S SYSTEM OF TRAILS

The fifty hikes described in this guide represent a cross-section of the 162-mile trail network in Mount Diablo State Park. They have been selected to help you explore the astonishing variety of environments that characterize the mountain. This variety is the result of the complex geology that has brought to us what we see and enjoy today, an isolated "island mountain" of surprising wilderness surrounded by broad valleys sheltering modern urban developments. And it is this ever-changing landscape, from deep stream-cut canyons to rocky summits, from flowery meadows to silent forests, that imparts to each trail its unique personality.

Trails in the guide include both double-track (dirt roads) and the more intimate single-track trails. Both are marked as such on the trail map of the park. The map, an indispensable companion to this guide book, is available at the park's visitor centers and entrance stations, and online at mdia.org. The trail system is actively maintained by park staff and trained volunteer groups, and the described trails should pose no undue hardship even to less experienced hikers. It should be emphasized, however, that, given the mountainous terrain, some of the more challenging trails are quite steep. A common difficulty, particularly on the dirt roads, is the presence of "ball bearings," small round pebbles, which can pose a footing problem. The more intimate trails, on the other hand, may become overgrown by vegetation in spite of the efforts of trail maintenance crews. Here the challenge may be one that is quite common in the Bay Area, the presence of poison oak and ticks. All of these hazards are avoidable with a modest amount of caution. Any unusual trail conditions are specified in the trail descriptions.

For the most part, however, trails are distinct and easy to follow. All trailheads and trail junctions are sign posted with trail names, destinations, and distances. With the help of these sign posts, this guide book, and the trails map, observant hikers will be likely to know their position at all times.

The park's trail system is available for multiple use—walkers, horses, and bicycles, with some restrictions. Horses are welcome on all trails except the Summit Trail above the Lower Summit parking lot/picnic area. However, the single-track trails often afford poor footing for horses, and the animals may be more comfortable on the network of double-track roads. Bicycles are restricted to the dirt roads, with the exception of several single-track trails that are provided as connectors within the road network. These "bikes-allowed" single-track trails are marked on the park map. Many roads are maintained as access roads for firefighters.

Multi-use trails can lead to some confusion among hikers, cyclists, and equestrians concerning right-of-way. Here are some simple guidelines. Cyclists must yield to hikers, preferably moving aside for the hikers. Cyclists and hikers must yield to equestrians, moving aside to allow them to pass. Equestrians recommend that cyclists and hikers speak or call out loudly to the equestrians before passing to reassure the horses. Let's share the trails and enjoy Mount Diablo State Park together.

How did Mount Diablo's trail system originate? Some of the roads are historical artifacts, such as Stage Road, built in 1874 as part of the connection from Martinez to the summit. Other roads are utility roads built to access various structures, installations, even resorts now long gone. But the majority of the roads were ranch roads, built to carry on the business of cattle management. Burma Road, named after the World War II supply route to China because of its mountainous resemblance to the original, was so named by Angel Kerley, matriarch of a cattle ranch within the confines of the park.

The single-track trails are even more varied in origin. Some were created by the park's administration. A notable example is Mary Bowerman Trail around the summit, which was built by the California Conservation Corps. Many trails, such as CCC Trail to the top of Sentinel Rock, were built by the Civilian Conservation Corps during the 1930s as part of the New Deal federal public relief program. Others were the handiwork of groups or individual trail enthusiasts, particularly in areas prior to incorporation into the state park. Falls Trail, for example, was the work of the legendary George Cardinet, founder of the California State Horsemen's Association, who declared, "Me and my horse did it." A few other trails in the park are remnants of long-ago mining activity.

And finally there are trails that are no longer there—the "Cinderellas." Some were purposely abandoned to protect fragile and rare natural resources; others faded away due to lack of maintenance or disuse. Trails considered too hazardous were occasionally closed by the park's administration. But the worst of the Cinderellas are various shortcuts or personal paths perpetrated by uncaring hikers or bikers. Scrambling down steep cliffs to the mountain's waterfalls does irreparable damage to the fragile environment, as does shortcutting of switchbacks. Although carefully stepping off the trail to explore an item of interest is acceptable, staying on the trail is the safest continuous action.

Anyone interested in the origin of some of Mount Diablo's colorful trail names may wish to consult the book, *Mountain Lore*, by Rich McDrew and Rachel Haislet, available in the park's visitor centers or online at mdia.org.

This guide is organized into five geographic locations that cover Mount Diablo State Park: North, South, Interior, West, and East. Within each geographic location, the hikes are arranged by trailhead. Hikes listed in the Interior section begin at or past the Junction Ranger Station along Summit Road, which means that you can enter the park from either the North Gate or the South Gate entrance to reach those trailheads.

Be sure to refer to the latest Trail Map of Mount Diablo State Park, an invaluable aid for hikers and other visitors to the park. In the hike descriptions, the location of the trailhead on the map grid is in parentheses, e.g., (J2) for the Mitchell Canyon Staging Area.

Each hike description consists of the following information:

Hike name | Hikes are usually named for a destination, prominent feature found along a hike, or the trails that the hike covers. Usually there are several ways to reach a destination, and several hikes reach the same destination from different trailheads or routes.

Distance | The distance is the hike's total mileage, and a notation indicates whether the hike is a round trip (out and back) or a loop. The mileage was calculated using data collected over many years by volunteers hiking in the park. As a general rule, a reasonably fit hiker covers two to three miles per hour on level ground, one to two miles per hour on gradual climbs, and about one mile per hour on the steepest climbs.

Difficulty | The terms easy, moderate, and strenuous are very subjective, factoring in distance, elevation gains and losses, trail conditions, and physical condition of the individual hikers. The distance in miles and cumulative climb in miles were multiplied and the numbers were divided into the following categories as general guidelines: easy, easy to moderate, moderate, moderate to strenuous, strenuous, and very strenuous.

Cumulative climb | This number is the elevation gain in feet when the trail is going uphill. This number is especially significant when the hike includes lots of ups and downs, for example, from peak to peak.

Trailhead | The name of the trailhead is identified, along with its grid location (letter and number in parentheses) on the Trail Map of Mount Diablo State Park. The trailheads for hikes in this book and the facilities at those trailheads are described in more detail at the beginning of each geographic section: North, South, Interior, West, and East.

Profile | A profile of the distance and elevation change gives you a quick visual representation of the hike, its basic ups and downs, and the distance covered.

Narrative | This section describes the general sequence of trails on the hike as well as what you may see along the trail: plants, animals, panoramic views, and perhaps some geologic and human history of the area.

Map | Each hike description is accompanied by a topographic map based on the seventh edition of the Trail Map of Mount Diablo State Park. The maps in this book are designed to convey the general direction of the hikes and should not be used as your sole source of map information. The Trail Map of Mount Diablo State Park provides detailed trail information.

Signature photo | The photo represents a significant feature of the hike or a typical environment.

In choosing a hike to match your ability, consider factors such as the mileage and elevation change as well as the condition of the trail, terrain, and season.

✳ STAYING SAFE

Getting lost, falling, hypothermia, and other unpleasant situations may happen when a hiker is not prepared. Here are just a few quick reminders for staying safe while hiking:

- Carry a trail map of Mount Diablo and know how to read it.
- Heed the trail signs.
- Be aware of where you are walking, especially if it is on loose rock, near a cliff, on a steep section of trail, or on slippery rocks or mud.
- Check the weather and dress appropriately. Wear layers. Wear sturdy walking/hiking shoes or boots. A hat and sunscreen are recommended, especially during the summer. Rain gear may be advisable in winter.
- Carry plenty of water and stay hydrated, especially during the hot summer months. Do not drink from streams or horse water troughs.
- Recognize the signs and symptoms of hypothermia (cold-related) and hyperthermia (heat-related) emergencies, and know how to administer emergency care if necessary, based on your comfort level.
- Keep track of the time. Remember that the park closes at sunset. Winter days are short, so plan carefully if you intend to go on a long hike. Let someone know where you are going and when you plan to return.
- Know your skill level and limitations.
- Learn to recognize poison oak, with its oak-like leaves in clusters of three, and stay away from it.
- Check often for ticks if hiking in areas known for harboring them, particularly on grassy, overgrown trails.

Poison Oak • Mike Woodring

- Use caution around rattlesnakes and know what to do in the unlikely situation that someone is bitten.

- A mountain lion is rarely seen on Mount Diablo, but if you do encounter one, don't run. Make yourself look big, stand your ground, and speak loudly.

This guide cannot cover every potential hazard you may encounter while you are hiking in Mount Diablo State Park. Describing the trails, roads, and natural features in this guide does not imply that they are safe or in the same condition as described in this publication. When you follow any of the hikes described in this guide, you assume responsibility for your own safety. Be sure to stay informed of the current weather, trail conditions, terrain, and other factors related to hiking these trails, and use common sense.

Remember, cell phones do not always work on the mountain, so do not rely on them.

- **Emergency:** Dial 911
- **Northern Dispatch (State Parks communications center for emergencies):** (916) 358-1300
- **Park closure and road conditions:** (925) 837-2525

✳ VISITING THE PARK

Mount Diablo State Park is open daily at 8 a.m. and closes at sunset. The gates are closed to arriving visitors at sunset; visitors should plan to be in their vehicles by early sunset and headed out to avoid being locked in.

Day use fees as of 2015 are as follows:

- **Main Entrances:** $10.00 per car
  Seniors 62 and over: $9.00 per car
- **Mitchell Canyon Staging Area:** $6.00 per car
  Seniors 62 and over: $5.00 per car
- **Macedo Ranch Staging Area:** $6.00 per car
  Seniors 62 and over: $5.00 per car

Annual passes are also available. Check the Mount Diablo State Park website, parks.ca.gov, or the Mount Diablo Interpretive Association website, mdia.org, for any changes to the fees or other regulations.

To date, California State Parks has completed hundreds of barrier removal and accessible trail projects statewide, including the accessible northern segment on the popular Mary Bowerman Trail. For current information regarding accessible features, including trails at Mount Diablo State Park, visitors are encouraged to call the park in advance at (925) 837-2525 or visit http://access.parks.ca.gov.

- All features of the park are protected. Do not remove or disturb plants, animals, or geological features.
- Dogs are not allowed on trails and fire roads.
- All alcoholic beverages are prohibited in the park.

Ask a park ranger for additional information regarding park rules and regulations.

Note: As of this printing, the information in this guide is as accurate as possible. Details about the park and the trails may change. Please contact the park or MDIA for the most up-to-date information.

- **Mount Diablo State Park:** (925) 837-2525 (general information), **parks.ca.gov**
- **MDIA:** (925) 927-2222 (voice mail), info@mdia.org

South Gate Entrance • Carl Nielson

Mitchell Canyon Road • Bill Karieva

NORTH TRAILHEADS

⚙ Mitchell Canyon Staging Area (J2)

Location: At the end of Mitchell Canyon Road, at the north entrance to the park, near the town of Clayton.

Parking: Ample, except on very busy days. Equestrian parking available.

Facilities: Drinking water, restrooms, park map display, picnic area, visitor center open on weekends, park headquarters nearby.

Day use fee: Payable at the "Iron Ranger" collection box at the entrance gate.

⚙ Regency Drive (K2)

Location: At the end of Regency Drive just east of the town of Clayton.

Parking: Adequate, on the street beyond the residences. The park gate is on the trail below, a short distance toward the mountain.

Facilities: Park map display.

Day use fee: Not collected.

Distance, difficulty: 4.0-mile round trip, easy to moderate
Cumulative climb: 930 feet
Trailhead: Mitchell Canyon Staging Area (J2)

Elevation in feet / Distance in miles

Mitchell Canyon • Dereck Love

Mitchell Canyon Road is a shaded, well-graded fire road, fairly level except for a slight rise and descent near the trailhead. Even a short jaunt into beautiful Mitchell Canyon is rewarding. The banks along the road display a wide variety of wildflowers from midwinter to spring's end. Dramatic outcrops of red rock loom high overhead, and your step will liven to the gentle watery tune of Mitchell Creek at trailside, well into late spring or early summer. The level part of the road is a marked nature trail; you can pick up a copy of the *Mitchell Canyon Interpretive Trail Guide* at the Mitchell Canyon Visitor Center and the trailhead. On sunny days, this is prime butterfly country. A copy of the *Butterfly List* is also available at the Mitchell Canyon Visitor Center.

It is one mile from ① the Mitchell Canyon staging area trailhead to the junction with Red Road, then another mile to ② where the road becomes steeper. Benches at trail intersections and a picnic table farther up the road reward weary hikers for their efforts. Complete the return loop by way of ❸ Globe Lily Trail, accessed just a few yards up Red Road. At ❹ its terminus, turn right and then left to get back onto Mitchell Canyon Road to return to the trailhead.

Mount Diablo Globe Lily
• Mike Woodring

Globe Lily Trail is named for the Mount Diablo globe lily, a beautiful near-endemic wildflower that is exceptionally prolific on the grassy slopes along the trail in spring.

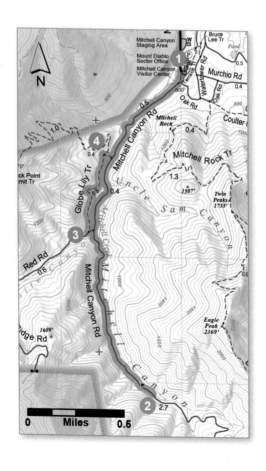

2 Mitchell Rock

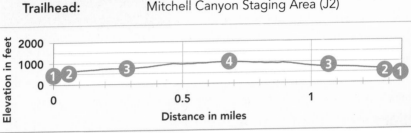

Distance, difficulty: 1.4-mile round trip, easy
Cumulative climb: 514 feet
Trailhead: Mitchell Canyon Staging Area (J2)

Mitchell Rock • Paul Salemme

This is deservedly one of the most popular walks on the mountain. Each step reveals novel views of the mountain's topography, neighboring towns, and distant bays. Mitchell Rock itself is a fascinating phenomenon, an outcrop of pillow lava transported to this site from the depths of the Pacific Ocean by tectonic activity.

A few yards beyond ① the Mitchell Canyon Road trailhead, ②
Oak Road takes off steeply to the left. In rainy weather, parts of Oak
Road can be very muddy. Once you reach the meadowy plateau at
the top, be on the lookout for ③ Mitchell Rock Trail, a single-track
trail to your right. This will take you all the way to your destination
of ④ Mitchell Rock, through a delightful environment of wildflowers
and flowering shrubs (with a few patches of poison oak off trail). You may
wish to cautiously climb to the top of the formation for even better views
and to admire the tough flowers that thrive on the inhospitable lava.

Return via the same route.

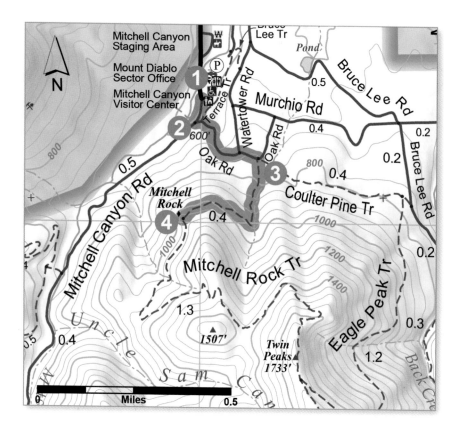

3 | The Northern Meadows

Distance, difficulty:	2.2-mile loop, easy
Cumulative climb:	364 feet
Trailhead:	Mitchell Canyon Staging Area (J2)

Oak Reflection in Pond along Bruce Lee Road • Joyce Chin

Highlights of this pleasant loop hike through the park's far northern meadowlands include a vigorous growth of Coulter pines, here at their northernmost limit, and, in spring, carpets of bright yellow Johnny jump-ups.

This hike begins at the northern end of the lower parking lot. Walk along ❶ Bruce Lee Road, which gently rises to the level of the meadows. The road meanders along, passing **2** a seasonal pond, and eventually turns toward the mountain's massif and Back Canyon, where a broad panorama of Mount Diablo's satellite peaks and canyons comes into view. The loop then meets **3** Coulter Pine Trail and continues along the length of this single-track trail to its meeting with **4** Oak Road. A sharp right on this road brings you to **5** Murchio Road, and a left here extends the loop to the slope at the edge of the meadows. Here you will spot a historic water tower to your right. Follow **6** Watertower Road to just beyond the tower where you will find the beginning of **7** Bruce Lee Trail on your left. Follow this back to the parking lot.

Some of the loop's roads pass over clay soil, which becomes very muddy in wet weather. In summer, lack of shade can render this hike uncomfortably warm.

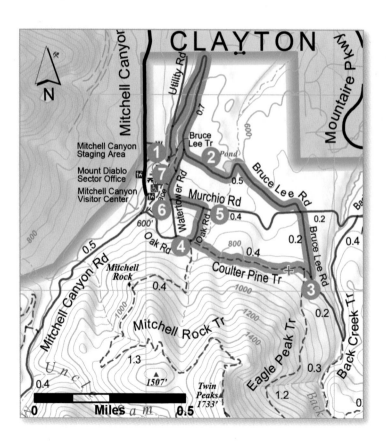

Distance, difficulty:	3.8-mile loop, moderate
Cumulative climb:	1,568 feet
Trailhead:	Mitchell Canyon Staging Area (J2)

Twin Peaks • Ray Mengel

This is a beautifully scenic loop at any time of the year, passing through several distinct habitat zones: meadowlands, oak savanna, chaparral, rocky summits, and a fine stand of Coulter pines.

Just a few yards beyond the Mitchell Canyon trailhead, a steep, but short, section of ❶ Oak Road begins. ❷ Mitchell Rock Trail is a single-track trail on your right that begins in the meadows above. The trail takes you past ③ Mitchell Rock, a fascinating island of pillow lava harboring delicate tundra-like flowers. Switchbacks bring you up to the lower of ④ the Twin Peaks. Pause to admire the brilliantly colored rocks at the peak and the venerable great-berried manzanitas, survivors of many fires, with exquisite blooms in January and February. Take care, the Twin Peaks area has dangerous vertical drop-offs! The trail continues to the upper Twin Peaks and, after a rough, rocky section, follows a gentle ridge with inspiring views. Be on the lookout for ⑤ Eagle Peak Trail where Mitchell Rock Trail ends. Take a left onto this trail to descend through scented chaparral to ⑥ Coulter Pine Trail, again on your left, in the meadows below. The final leg of the loop lets you admire the Coulter pines, here at the northern limit of their habitat, and in mid-spring, fine displays of Johnny jump-ups in the undergrowth.

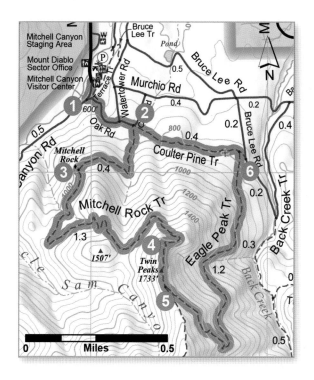

5 Black Point

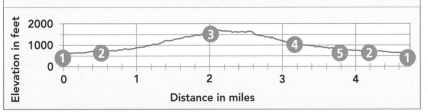

Distance, difficulty: 4.7-mile loop, moderate
Cumulative climb: 1,635 feet
Trailhead: Mitchell Canyon Staging Area (J2)

Black Point • Ray Mengel

This hike highlights a less frequently traveled corner of the park, spanning several life zones. During late summer and early autumn around dusk, the first half-mile or so of Black Point Trail is a popular location for spotting male tarantulas wandering about in search of females with which to mate. Please do not disturb the gentle giants or their webbed burrows.

The hike begins at ① the Mitchell Canyon trailhead. ② Black Point Trail proper starts about one-half mile along Mitchell Canyon Road, on the right beyond the creek crossing. ③ A short side trail takes you to the chaparral-covered summit of Black Point. During the descent from Black Point, watch for trailside "glory holes," exploratory tunnels dug to establish the existence of a promising mineral lode. The Black Point Trail ends on ④ Red Road, and the loop is completed by taking ⑤ Mitchell Canyon Road back to the trailhead. You may return instead via Globe Lily Trail, which parallels the road. In spring, fine displays of the near-endemic Mount Diablo globe lily can often be seen on this trail.

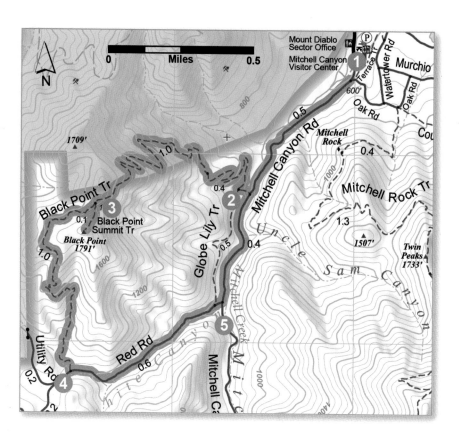

6 | Olofson Ridge

Distance, difficulty: 5.4-mile round trip, moderate
Cumulative climb: 1,630 feet
Trailhead: Mitchell Canyon Staging Area (J2)

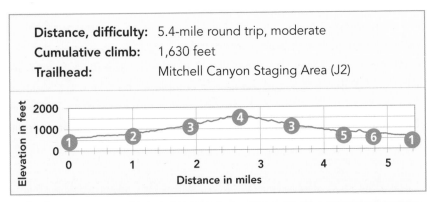

Moon Rising over Olofson Ridge • Bill Karieva

The highlight of this hike is the opportunity to enjoy the awe-inspiring chasm of Mitchell Canyon and the massive walls of Eagle Peak from a unique perspective.

Begin the hike at ① the Mitchell Canyon trailhead. After hiking one mile along beautiful Mitchell Canyon, turn right on ② Red Road, which, incongruously, climbs White Canyon. In springtime, this is the site of rarer wildflower species such as the Mount Diablo globe lily and wind poppies. Take a sharp left onto ❸ Olofson Ridge Road. After a steady but gentle climb for three quarters of a mile, you reach ❹ the park boundary gate; turn left up and over a slight rise to the left (east) of the trail. Find yourself a perch on a rocky outcrop. From this vista point, you can lose yourself in the world of hawks, kestrels, and turkey vultures. With luck, you may even spot a golden eagle.

On the trip back, check out ❺ Globe Lily Trail, reached just a few yards before Red Road intersects with Mitchell Canyon Road. Globe Lily Trail is named after the Mount Diablo globe lily, a beautiful near-endemic wildflower; it is exceptionally prolific on the grassy slopes along the trail in springtime. At ❻ the trail's terminus, turn right to reach Mitchell Canyon Road, then left to return to the trailhead.

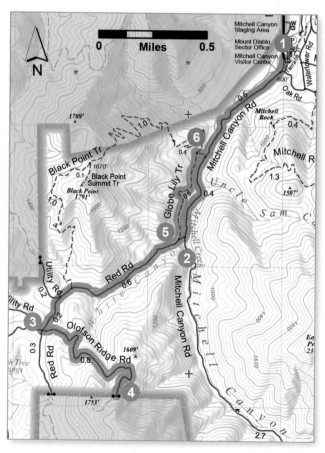

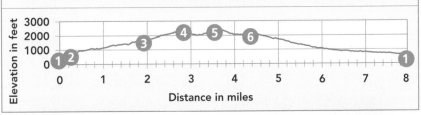

Distance, difficulty: 8.0-mile loop, strenuous
Cumulative climb: 3,101 feet
Trailhead: Mitchell Canyon Staging Area (J2)

Eagle Peak Trail • Carl Nielson

This loop is a favorite hike that docents at the Mitchell Canyon Visitor Center often recommend as an introduction to first-time hikers in the park who want great views and a variety of habitats, along with a good workout.

Follow Mitchell Canyon Road to ❶ Oak Road, which takes off steeply to the left where the split rail fencing ends. After you reach the meadowy plateau at the top, look for ❷ Mitchell Rock Trail, a single-track trail to your right. This will take you past Mitchell Rock and Twin Peaks to ③ Eagle Peak Trail, an exciting ridge trail, often only a few feet wide, with sharp drop-offs on each side. This trail leads, of course, to ④ Eagle Peak. Eagle Peak is a rocky belvedere from which to admire the expanse of Contra Costa's "Central Valley" before you, and a good place to pause for a break on several rocks nature has conveniently placed for this purpose. Continue on to ⑤ Murchio Gap, and take Meridian Ridge Road to the right to reach Deer Flat. At Deer Flat, continue to the right on ⑥ Mitchell Canyon Road for a short distance to find picnic tables in the shade and a restful place to enjoy Deer Flat, one of the mountain's loveliest spots, with its symphony of bird song. Mitchell Canyon Road takes you back to the trailhead. Your return via shady Mitchell Canyon offers a welcome relief from the heat of the afternoon sun.

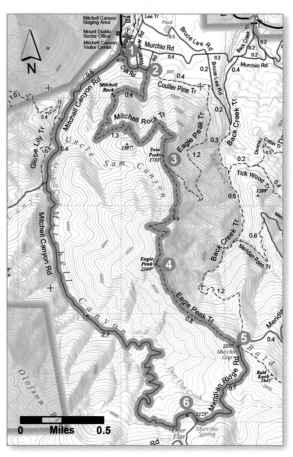

8 Little Giant Loop

Distance, difficulty: 9.4-mile round trip, strenuous
Cumulative climb: 3,202 feet
Trailhead: Mitchell Canyon Staging Area (J2)

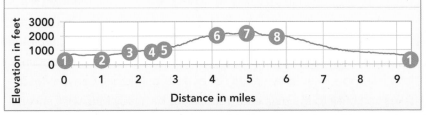

Deer on Tick Wood Trail • Joyce Chin

This is a shorter version of the Giant Loop described in Hike #9 in this guide. The Little Giant Loop is exceptional in spring, with its mass wildflower display.

A little beyond the gate at the trailhead where the split rail fencing ends, turn left and follow ① Oak and Murchio roads eastward through the foothill meadows to ② Back Creek Trail. Turn right and follow Back

Creek Trail to ③ Tick Wood Trail. Spring rains make for soggy footing, but the mysterious oak groves with emerald grassy carpets make the effort worthwhile. This path takes you to ④ Donner Canyon Road, and a right turn soon brings you to Meridian Ridge Road. Follow this road to ⑤ Middle Trail, a fragile ecological treasure. Continue on Middle Trail, which climbs up to ⑥ Prospectors Gap Road. Turn right to meet Meridian Ridge Road, and continue left to Murchio Gap, where several trails meet. Take ⑦ Meridian Ridge Road to reach Deer Flat. At the Deer Flat intersection, continue to the right on ⑧ Mitchell Canyon Road for a short distance to find picnic tables in the shade and a restful place to enjoy lovely Deer Flat and a chorus of bird song. After a series of rocky switchbacks, Mitchell Canyon Road offers a shady respite from the sun most of the way back to the trailhead.

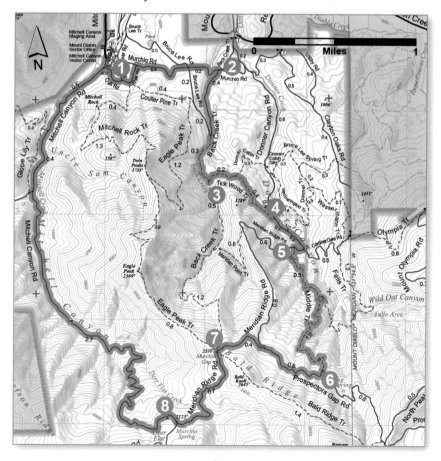

9 Summit via Back Creek (Giant Loop)

Distance, difficulty:	12.6-mile round trip, very strenuous
Cumulative climb:	4,746 feet
Trailhead:	Mitchell Canyon Staging Area (J2)

Back Creek Cascades • Ray Mengel

Circumnavigating the mountain, this is the definitive Mount Diablo hike, encompassing all of the park's life zones, from meadowlands to rocky summit. The ever-changing views are simply stunning, well worth the considerable effort required to complete this rewarding hike.

Follow Mitchell Canyon Road a short distance to ① Oak Road where the split rail fencing ends. Turn left. After reaching the meadowy plateau, continue to ② Coulter Pine Trail. From Coulter Pine Trail, turn onto Bruce Lee Road, which intersects with ③ Back Creek Trail. Continue on Back Creek Trail to Meridian Ridge Road at Murchio Gap, where several trails meet. Across Meridian Ridge Road is the beginning of ④ Bald Ridge Trail. Continue on Bald Ridge Trail until it ends at Prospectors Gap. Take ⑤ North Peak Trail and circle the summit until

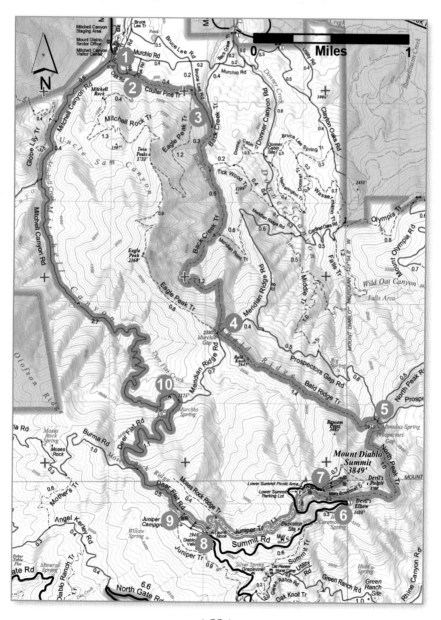

you reach **6** Devil's Elbow near Summit Road. Look for Summit Trail heading up to the right. Summit Trail takes you to the Lower Summit Picnic Area and continues a short distance uphill between the one-way paved roads to and from the summit. **7** The summit itself is inside the Visitor Center rotunda.

Return via Summit Trail to the Lower Summit Picnic Area. Follow Juniper Trail across the parking lot to its west end and continue down to **8** Juniper Campground. Pass through Laurel Nook Group Picnic Area and take the road to the right until reaching the far end of the campground. Continue on **9** Deer Flat Road to Deer Flat and its intersection with **10** Mitchell Canyon Road, which takes you back to the trailhead.

Coulter Pine Trail • Joyce Chin

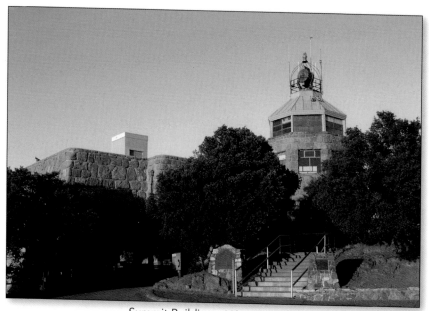

Summit Building • Mike Woodring

A popular variation to this hike goes up Mitchell Rock Trail and Eagle Peak Trail instead of Back Creek Trail. Expect to climb an additional 500 feet for the spectacular bird's eye view from Eagle Peak.

View from Eagle Peak • Jack McKeown

10 Five Peaks Trek

Distance, difficulty: 14.5-mile loop, very strenuous
Cumulative climb: 6,280 feet
Trailhead: Mitchell Canyon Staging Area (J2)

View of Summit from North Peak Trail • Paul Salemme

This hike is for hardy adventurers eager to conquer the park's five major peaks in one day. With peaks as the objective, scenic views naturally become the highlight, and these are ever-changing and truly inspiring. The Five Peaks epic circuit consists largely of single-track trails, which contribute to the wilderness aspect of your adventure.

The usual sequence starts at ❶ the Mitchell Canyon trailhead and takes in ❷ Twin Peaks, ❸ Eagle Peak, ❹ Mount Diablo's main peak,

⑤ North Peak, and ⑥ Mount Olympia, in that order, with a return to Mitchell Canyon. Experience in map reading and navigation is essential for this hike; be sure to carry the Trail Map of Mount Diablo State Park. Depending on the itinerary you pick, you must be ready to cover nearly 15 miles and several climbs totaling more than 6,200 feet. Clearly, this is a trek for experienced hikers in good physical condition.

If you wish to go even farther and hit all the peaks in the park, try this sequence: Start at the Mitchell Canyon trailhead and go to Mount Diablo's main peak, North Peak, Mount Olympia, Eagle Peak, and Twin Peaks, in that order. Return to Mitchell Canyon Road and continue on to Black Point before returning to the Mitchell Canyon trailhead.

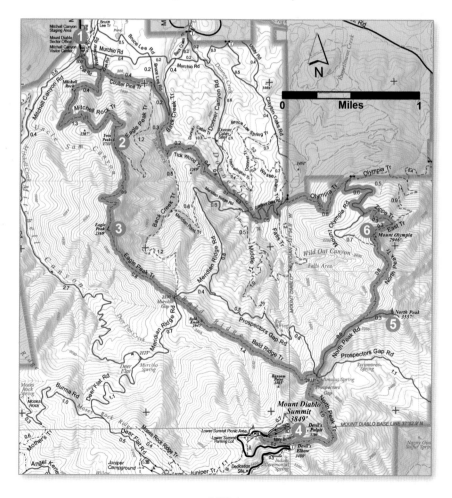

11 | Donner Creek

Distance, difficulty: 1.8-mile round trip, easy
Cumulative climb: 316 feet
Trailhead: Regency Drive (K2)

Donner Canyon Road • Joyce Chin

The attractive environment of Donner Canyon is dominated by the view of the park's principal peaks, rising sharply from the meadows at the base. In spring, the sight of the rushing waters of Donner Creek flowing through flower-strewn emerald green grasslands is unforgettable.

Begin this easy walk on level ① Donner Canyon Road, which is popular with local residents, families with strollers, joggers, and kids on bikes. The road gently transitions from open grasslands to an oak savanna into a riparian environment, thereafter reaching the site of ➋ Donner Cabin, an early pioneer residence, where you can turn around to return to the trailhead, or continue walking to extend the distance. Interesting side trails off the fire road invite additional exploration.

This beautiful canyon and the cabin were named for John Donner and his descendants. According to the 1880 census in Clayton, John was born in 1814 in Canada. John and his family developed a farm in the area of Donner Canyon in the 1870s. He was not a member of the ill-fated Donner Party that came to California in the 1840s.

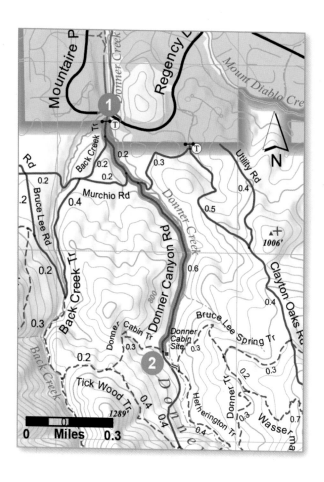

Distance, difficulty: 3.1-mile loop, easy
Cumulative climb: 761 feet
Trailhead: Regency Drive (K2)

Bruce Lee Spring Trail • Paul Salemme

This short but sometimes steep climb partway up the north side of the mountain features sweeping views, abundant wildflowers, and opportunities for wildlife viewing.

Follow ❶ Donner Canyon Road to ❷ the signpost directing you to Clayton Oaks Road on the left. Rock-hop across Donner Creek and ascend the hills to enjoy views of grassy meadows and stately oaks, as well as Mount Olympia, North Peak, and the Summit. The first poppies of early spring appear here in February or March, followed by a progression of wildflowers through summer. A herd of does can sometimes be seen along the ridge to the left of the trail ascending from Donner Canyon. When the fall and winter rains bring green grass, the deer descend to the fire road to graze on the delicate seedlings. Follow Clayton Oaks Road to its intersection with ③ Bruce Lee Spring Trail on the right. Wind your way through the chaparral—heavenly scented black sage, yerba santa, and California sagebrush. Follow Bruce Lee Spring Trail to ④ Hetherington Trail and turn right. In spring, you'll encounter a plethora of violets, owl's clover, and milkmaids. In summer, golden grasses oscillate in the breeze.

After a very short descent to the creek along Donner Canyon, cross the footbridge or rock-hop to return to Donner Canyon Road and the trailhead.

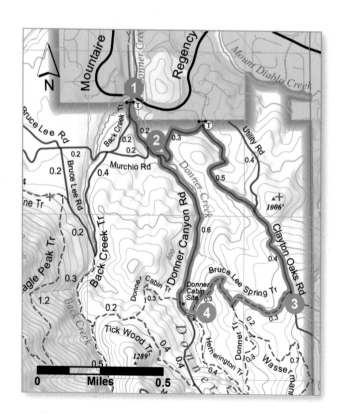

13 Hetherington, Meridian Point, Back Creek Trails

Distance, difficulty: 4.4-mile loop, moderate

Cumulative climb: 1,451 feet

Trailhead: Regency Drive (K2)

Meridian Point Trail • Mike Woodring

This short and occasionally steep hike takes you through some of the most beautiful scenery on the mountain and offers the chance to spot some of the mountain's wildlife.

Start at ❶ Regency Gate, and follow Donner Canyon Road to the former site of Donner Cabin on the left. From late spring to early fall, families of quails may appear before the Donner Cabin gate in late afternoon. Turn left onto ❷ Hetherington Trail to the first creek crossing.

In spring, you may spot a mother mallard and her ducklings in the creek. Continue along Hetherington Trail, crossing Donner Creek again, and follow it through the forested and fragrant chaparral. Starting in January, abundant wildflowers and bushes bloom here—manzanita, milkmaids, buttercups, hound's tongue, followed by shooting stars and Mount Diablo globe lilies in spring. In summer, this trail offers shady respite from heat. In fall, you'll find native grapes here.

Turn left at the southern intersection with ③ Donner Canyon Road, and continue to the intersection of ④ Meridian Ridge Road. Turn right onto Meridian Ridge Road, and follow it to the intersection of ⑤ Meridian Point Trail. Turn right on Meridian Point Trail, and descend, through more wildflowers and lush black sage, to ⑥ Back Creek Trail. Turn right on Back Creek Trail—more chaparral and wildflowers and the occasional deer, hawk, butterfly, lizard, and great horned owl—to return to Donner Canyon Road and back to Regency Gate, perhaps witnessing the presence of the resident wild turkey flock.

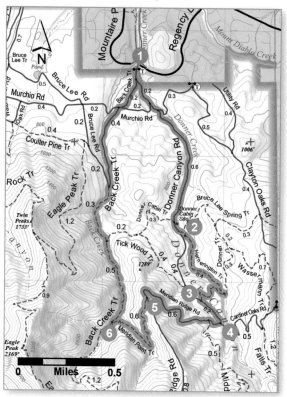

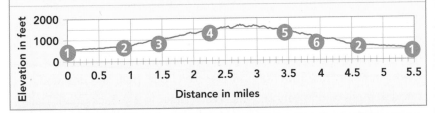

Distance, difficulty:	5.5-mile loop, moderate to strenuous
Cumulative climb:	2,020 feet
Trailhead:	Regency Drive (K2)

Falls Trail Water Boulders • Paul Salemme

In the rainy winter season and throughout spring, Falls Trail offers fine views of several waterfalls and cascades. Spring also brings astounding displays of wildflowers, and the colorful rock formations are worth the trip any time of the year.

    Beyond the trailhead gate, follow ❶ Donner Canyon Road to the former site of Donner Cabin. Just beyond, turn left onto ❷ Hetherington

Trail to cross Donner Creek. After a few steps along Hetherington Trail, take Bruce Lee Spring Trail (left), Donner Trail (right), and  Wassermann Trail (left) to Cardinet Oaks Road. A short distance to the right is the start of ❹ Falls Trail on the left side of the road. Please refrain from scrambling around the falls as this is dangerous for people and damaging to the landscape. Falls Trail, in turn, ends at ❺ Middle Trail, a fragile ecological treasure with an abundance of fragrant chamise and black sage. Turn right and follow Middle Trail, to its end at ❻ Meridian Ridge Road. Turn right and then left onto Donner Canyon Road. Take Donner Canyon Road back to the trailhead.

Diablo Falls • Bill Karieva

While the hike is not difficult, some stream crossings may be steep and slippery. In winter and early spring, the roads and trails may be muddy, so allow extra time for the hike.

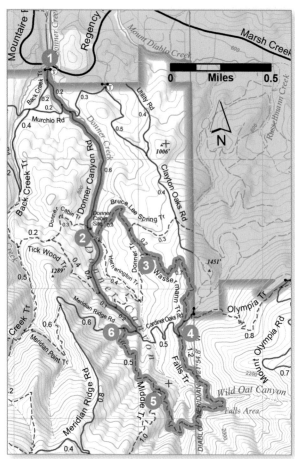

Mount Olympia via Donner Canyon Road

Distance, difficulty:	9.5-mile loop, strenuous
Cumulative climb:	4,050 feet
Trailhead:	Regency Drive (K2)

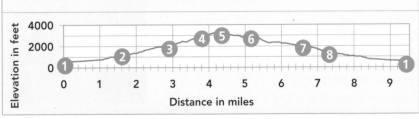

Mount Olympia • Dereck Love

Mount Olympia is one of the park's prime destinations, a rugged outcrop with fantastic views of dizzying canyons, particularly with the mists of winter.

Follow **1** Donner Canyon Road to Meridian Ridge Road on the right. After a short distance, turn left onto **2** Middle Trail, a nature lover's delight, which takes you to **3** Prospectors Gap Road. Turn left and begin the very steep and challenging climb to ④ Prospectors Gap. Consider a brief respite at Big Spring along the way, but beware of the plentiful poison oak. At Prospectors Gap, turn left to follow North Peak Road. Notice the 2013 fire devastation from the right side of the road. Continue left onto ⑤ North Peak Trail, which takes you to ⑥ Mount Olympia, where you can record your success in the summit register attached to the trail post. Continue the loop by going down Mount Olympia Road and turning left onto ⑦ Olympia Trail (avoid private property). Return along ⑧ Cardinet Oaks Road to the previously traversed Donner Canyon Road, finally retracing your steps to the trailhead.

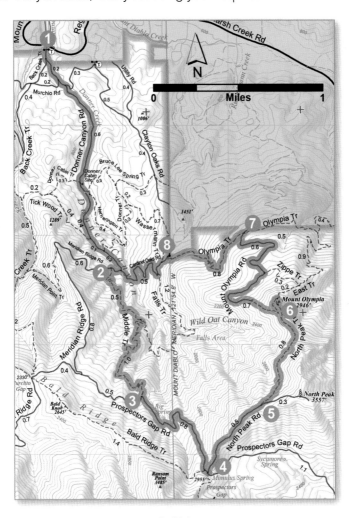

Rock City
• Carl Nielson

 ## Curry Point (K10)

Location: At the pullout on the east side of South Gate Road at an elevation of 1,780 feet, beyond Rock City going uphill.

Parking: Ample at the large parking pullout.

Facilities: Park map display. Nearest facilities are at Rock City.

Day use fee: Collected at the South Gate and North Gate entrance stations.

 ## Lower Rock City (J10)

Location: In Rock City along South Gate Road at an elevation of 1,620 feet, less than a mile beyond the South Gate entrance station going uphill.

Parking: Limited. Park at the side of the paved loop road near the restrooms. Other parking spaces may be available at various locations in Rock City.

Facilities: Drinking water, restrooms, park map display, picnic area, campground nearby.

Day use fee: Collected at the South Gate and North Gate entrance stations.

⚙ Uplands Picnic Area (J10)

Location: Near the southern entrance to Rock City at an elevation of 1,620 feet, adjacent to South Gate Road, at the junction with a small side road to Live Oak Campground.

Parking: Limited. Other parking spaces may be available at various locations in Rock City.

Facilities: Drinking water, Lower Rock City restrooms and park map display nearby, picnic area, campground nearby.

Day use fee: Collected at the South Gate and North Gate entrance stations.

⚙ Macedo Ranch Staging Area (F8)

Location: At the end of Green Valley Road in Alamo. Green Valley Road may be reached from Stone Valley Road or Diablo Road, both Interstate 680 exits.

Parking: Ample. Equestrian parking available.

Facilities: Drinking water, restrooms, park map display, picnic area, horse water trough and hose.

Day use fee: Payable at the "Iron Ranger" collection box in the parking lot.

⚙ Finley Road (Q14)

Location: From Interstate 680 in Danville, take Sycamore Valley Road east to reach Camino Tassajara. Continue east on Camino Tassajara for seven miles to Finley Road. Turn left onto Finley Road. Roadside parking is at the north end of Finley Road, about two miles from Camino Tassajara.

Parking: Parking is not allowed at the trailhead; park along the roadside beyond the "No Parking" signs, about three quarters of a mile from the trailhead.

Facilities: None.

Day use fee: Not collected.

16 | Camp Force Overlook

Distance, difficulty:	0.7-mile round trip, easy
Cumulative climb:	203 feet
Trailhead:	Curry Point (K10)

Camp Force Overlook • Dereck Love

This delightful short excursion is a prime opportunity for visitors driving through the park to stop briefly and enjoy a wilderness experience. The intimate single-track Camp Force Trail meanders across flower-strewn meadows and through oak groves. Many years ago this was the site of a Boy Scout camp (Camp Force), abandoned due to the park's strict fire regulations—for what is a Boy Scout camp without a roaring camp fire? The only remaining traces of the Scout presence are a couple of crumbling stone stoves.

As you face east near the beginning of the wide Curry Canyon Road, ➊ Camp Force Trail, a single-track trail marked with its own trail post, is on the right, to the right of the posted Mount Diablo map display.

On the way in on your left, you may notice ➋ a metal plaque set in a sandstone boulder, a 1954 memorial honoring Boy Scouts and Raymond Force, the gentleman responsible for creating the camp.

The short trail ends at ➌ an overlook offering a spectacular bird's-eye view of Gibraltar Rock and other formations across Madrone Canyon. These are favorites of local rock climbers, and, with luck, you might spot some of them on the cliff faces. A low stone wall at the overlook is a good resting spot to enjoy the view and the magic of this ridge-top site. In early spring, manzanitas are in full bloom, with carpets of red Indian warriors at their base.

17 Garden of the Jungle Gods

Distance, difficulty: 3.4-mile loop, easy to moderate
Cumulative climb: 1,044 feet
Trailhead: Curry Point (K10)

Rock City Wind Caves • Roi Peers

In the distant past, Garden of the Jungle Gods was a name given to the Rock City area, a name that has now faded from common use. But the loop trail is, indeed, a walk through a Garden of the Gods, with delightful surprises around each corner.

Begin this captivating loop hike on ① Curry Canyon Road, continuing to the right onto ② Knobcone Point Road where you will enjoy fine views and magnificent old oaks, which are particularly picturesque when shrouded in winter's fog. Descend on ❸ Devil's Slide Trail on the right to a riparian environment of deep canyons and pungent sulfur springs, then turn right again and follow ❹ Madrone Canyon Trail, where you can admire the stately madrone trees with their peeling red bark as the trail gradually rises to the Rock City area. At the end of the trail, across South Gate Road, ❺ Rock City Trail begins. This trail features several points of interest, including wildly eroded rock formations, wind caves, and Native American grinding holes.

At the junction with Civilian Conservation Corps (CCC) Trail, if you wish, you can undertake the rock scramble leading to Sentinel Rock (see Hike 22, Sentinel Rock). Rock City Trail ends at the intersection of Wall Point Road and Summit Trail. Turn right and take ❻ Summit Trail to Staircase Trail. At the upper end of Staircase Trail, turn right again to continue on ❼ Summit Trail and then Camp Force Trail to return to the Curry Point trailhead. Reference to the Trail Map of Mount Diablo State Park is strongly recommended.

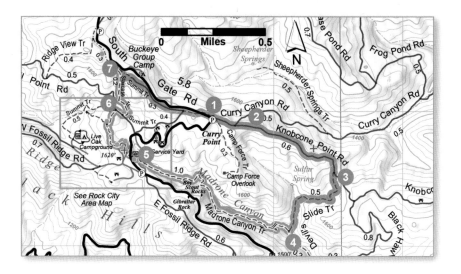

18 | Balancing Rock and Knobcone Point

Distance, difficulty: 4.1-mile round trip, easy to moderate
Cumulative climb: 1,079 feet
Trailhead: Curry Point (K10)

Balancing Rock • Kevin Hintsa

This mostly level hike offers a couple of especially interesting park features: a healthy stand of knobcone pine trees and the gravity-defying Balancing Rock.

From ① the trailhead, follow Curry Canyon Road to the point where Knobcone Point Road veers to the right, and continue on ② Knobcone Point Road. After another ¾ mile or so, keep to the left at ③ the "Y" in the road where Black Hawk Ridge Road begins to the right. Knobcone Point Road follows the crest of the tilted strata of Domengine sandstone. Along the way, enjoy a serene rest stop at the beautiful redwood picnic table partially hidden on the left side of the road, placed there in memory of longtime park volunteer Kate McKillop (1936-2009). Further along the road, note the uniform stand of knobcone pines on and around Knobcone Point. Because the cones of knobcone pines only open when exposed to intense heat, knobcone pines require fire for regeneration. A 1997 prescribed fire near Knobcone Point was directed at the knobcone forest and expanse of chaparral that had no record of fire in the past century. Near the end of Knobcone Point Road is the massive eroded sandstone teetering wall known as ④ Balancing Rock, perched precariously along the side of the road. This feature has been faithfully reproduced on a

Knobcone Pine • Kevin Hintsa

full scale and forms the display focus at Walnut Creek's Lindsay Wildlife Museum.

A short distance beyond Balancing Rock is ⑤ a park boundary gate. Retrace your steps to the trailhead.

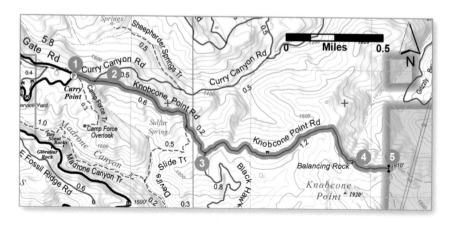

19 Oyster Point from Curry Point

Distance, difficulty:	7.5-mile round trip, strenuous
Cumulative climb:	2,402 feet
Trailhead:	Curry Point (K10)

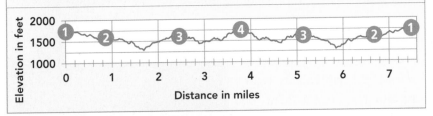

View from Oyster Point • Mike Woodring

The scenery on this hike is constantly changing and is a source of unending delight: meadow wildflowers in the spring, fall colors in the depths of Sycamore Canyon, and the fantastic Domengine sandstone formations to the east of Knobcone Point at any time of the year.

Begin by following ① Curry Canyon Road to Knobcone Point Road, then right to ② Black Hawk Ridge Road. On Black Hawk Ridge Road, descend into Sycamore Canyon, and then climb again until you reach ③ Oyster Point Trail. Follow this until you reach ④ an informal trail to your right, marked by a trail sign below the summit of Oyster Point.

You may wish to undertake the steep scramble to the summit, but there is no official trail—and lots of poison oak. The summit is a Miocene sandstone hogback, where you may perch on a rock of your choice to view the glorious panorama of San Ramon and the Bay Area beyond, and, in the opposite direction, the wilderness of Jackass Canyon far below. Look closely and you may spot fossils of oysters, for which the point was named.

Retrace your steps to the trailhead.

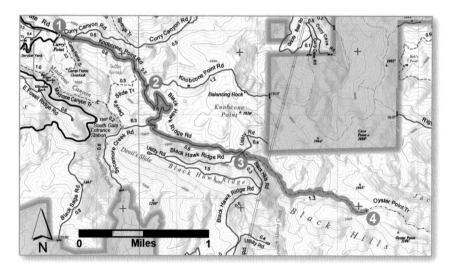

20 Loop Hike into History

Distance, difficulty:	7.7-mile round trip, strenuous
Cumulative climb:	2,409 feet
Trailhead:	Curry Point (K10)

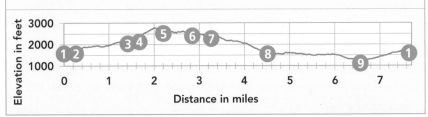

View from Curry Point • Mike Woodring

In addition to traversing different habitats, this hike passes through various points of historical interest in the park.

From ➊ Curry Point, go west and walk beside South Gate Road. Cross at the crosswalk, and continue uphill on ➋ Summit Trail. A Trail Through Time (TTT) interpretive panel along the way describes how Mount Diablo was formed 190 million years ago. Again cross South

Gate Road and proceed uphill on Summit Trail. A short distance uphill you will pass another TTT panel describing a major thrust fault along which the core rocks of the mountain have been pushed up and over younger rocks. Continue uphill another half mile to ❸ the Sunset Picnic Area (pit toilets and drinking water here). The rock masonry work on the "Diablo Stove" and picnic table/bench pedestals were crafted by the Civilian Conservation Corps (CCC) in the 1930s.

Cross Summit Road and continue uphill on Summit Trail. In the field behind a park residence on the left is a structure with a smokestack: an oven used by the CCC to heat asphalt for roofing and road topping. Slightly farther up the Summit Trail is ❹ the historic Mountain House site. Mountain House was the first and only hotel that was built on Mount Diablo. It opened for business in 1874, closed in 1891, and burned completely in 1901, so nothing physical remains today. Continue uphill on Summit Trail. Cross Summit Road and on the right take Oak Knoll Trail through the chaparral to ❺ the Oak Knoll Picnic Area.

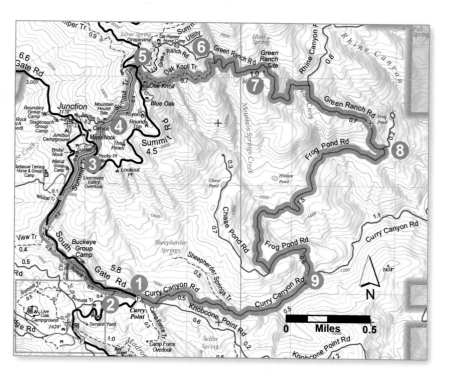

Continue on Oak Knoll Trail to ⑥ Green Ranch Road. Turn right and in about one-half mile you will arrive at ⑦ Green Ranch, a 170-acre parcel held by Robert and Deborah Green from 1938 to 1965. The Greens with their four children built a summer house, now demolished. Locate the wall-less living room by the still-standing fireplace and enjoy the southern exposure and beautiful view.

Continue on Green Ranch Road to ⑧ Frog Pond Road, then turn right and continue to ⑨ Curry Canyon Road. Turn right on Curry Canyon Road and go about 100 yards to an unmarked volunteer trail on the left. Take that trail up 25 yards to a Native American grinding rock site, one of the most popular grinding rock locations for Native Americans as far back as 5,000 years ago.

While trekking up Curry Canyon Road, notice remnants of homesteading (non-native trees) and cattle ranching (cattle loading platform). Continue uphill to Curry Point and the trailhead.

Consider reversing the direction of this hike during the dry season. Green Ranch Road has some steep sections and loose gravel that may be easier to traverse when hiking uphill rather than down.

Diablo Stove • Dereck Love

Still-Standing Fireplace at Green Ranch Site • Debbie McKeown

Native American Grinding Holes • Mike Woodring

Distance, difficulty:	17.2-mile loop, very strenuous
Cumulative climb:	5,501 feet
Trailhead:	Curry Point (K10)

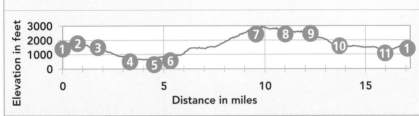

Reeds in Pine Pond • Bill Karieva

Experienced hikers are rewarded with ever-changing scenery and an exhilarating scramble up and down the flanks of the mountain. When it's time for a break, grab a shady seat beside one of the two ponds along this hike, Frog Pond or Pine Pond.

From ❶ Curry Point, go west and parallel South Gate Road on the single-track Camp Force Trail. Cross at the crosswalk, and continue uphill on Summit Trail. Follow this sequence of trails: Summit Trail to

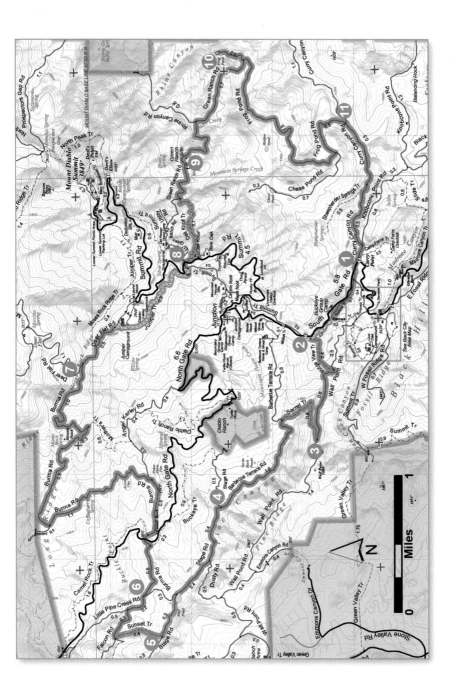

2 Ridge View Trail to Wall Point Road to **3** the lovely forested Secret Trail, considered by some to be one of the prettiest single-track trails in the park. After a gentle descent on Secret Trail, continue down Pine Canyon on to Barbecue Terrace Road, then to **4** Stage Road and, in

Secret Trail • Paul Salemme

less than a mile, to Pine Pond. The pond, almost completely silted up, is a haven for numerous bird species. A word of warning: Rattlesnakes are regulars in Pine Canyon, especially by Pine Pond.

Beyond Pine Pond, take **5** Sunset Trail to Falcon Road, Little Pine Creek Road, and **6** Burma Road. Burma Road offers a bracing ascent, a worthy challenge midway through this rewarding hike. Landowner Angel Kerley chose the name Burma Road after the original road of the same name in Burma to acknowledge the challenging engineering feat to construct this road through the steep terrain of Mount Diablo. The sweeping views should divert your attention from this heart-pumping climb.

Continue on Burma Road all the way to **7** Deer Flat Road and its end near Juniper Campground. At the auto gate, turn right to follow the lower section of Juniper Trail, a short section of Summit Trail, **8** Oak Knoll Trail, and Green Ranch Road to **9** the Green Ranch site. Green Ranch Road descends to its end on Frog Pond Road; here make a short side trip to **10** Frog Pond. Linger at Frog Pond and you may be lucky enough to hear the oddly musical song of its namesake inhabitants.

Return along Frog Pond Road and continue to its terminus on **11** Curry Canyon Road. A right onto Curry Canyon Road takes you back to the trailhead.

To accommodate the time span required for this long hike during daylight hours, late spring or early fall are the best seasons. This challenging hike requires expert map reading skills. Refer to the trail map of the park to find shortcuts to this loop if necessary.

Burma Road and Deer Flat Road Junction • Dereck Love

Frog Pond • Mike Woodring

Distance, difficulty:	0.8-mile round trip, easy
Cumulative climb:	322 feet
Trailhead:	Lower Rock City (J10)

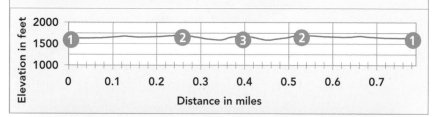

Sentinel Rock • Carl Nielson

This short hike features a wonderland of sandstone formations, Native American grinding holes, and the famous wind caves.

Begin on ① Rock City Trail, and at the junction with ② Civilian Conservation Corps Trail, turn left and proceed along the trail to a large, smooth rock with carved steps for fine views of Sentinel Rock and the valley beyond. Well-conditioned adults and happy kids may continue to ③ Sentinel Rock itself, the tallest rock in Rock City. Be aware that no actual trail exists—just a lot of climbing and scrambling over slippery rock formations. A carved, very rough stairway takes you to the top of Sentinel Rock, a climb aided by cables. At the top, enjoy the spectacular view of Mount Diablo's summit while staying safely behind the cable barriers.

One of the most notable features of the Rock City area is its wind caves. These weirdly eroded sandstone caves are not created by wind but rather through the effect of seasonal rainfall. Seepage through the rock removes much of the material cementing the sand grains together. The loose sands are ultimately removed by surface erosion, creating holes in the rocks that gradually enlarge to form caves.

For another perspective on this fascinating area, hikers might consider exploring the section of Summit Trail that passes the base of Sentinel Rock. Access Summit Trail from either Live Oak Campground or Wall Point Road.

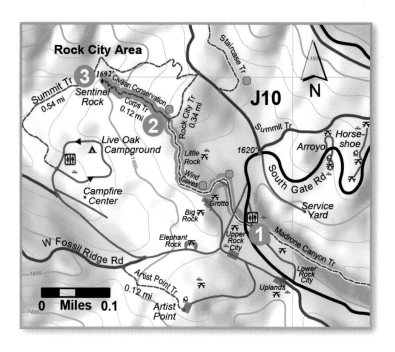

23 East Fossil Ridge

Distance, difficulty: 1.3-mile round trip, easy
Cumulative climb: 318 feet
Trailhead: Uplands Picnic Area (J10)

View from East Fossil Ridge • Mike Woodring

The initial short, steep climb up ❶ East Fossil Ridge Road opens up to imposing, ever-changing vistas of the massive main peak of the mountain, San Ramon Valley, and the rugged wilderness to the east. On clear days, Sacramento Valley is visible in the distance. East Fossil Ridge Road parallels the crest of Fossil Ridge and is partially shaded along the way. ❷ The end of the road is marked by an "End of Trail" sign.

A well-defined but unofficial trail starts at the "End of Trail" sign and leads through an area where some of the stones used for building the Summit Visitor Center were quarried. Remains of the boulders, with a few fossils, may still be found in the underbrush. Outcrops at the top of the ridge are full of similar fossils, mostly marine shells (clams and oysters).

The overlook spot at the end of the unofficial trail offers a dramatic view of Black Hawk Ridge strata across Sycamore Canyon and a bird's eye view of Devil's Slide. This is a good bird watching location.

Distance, difficulty:	4.6-mile loop, moderate
Cumulative climb:	1,621 feet
Trailhead:	Lower Rock City (J10)

Secret Trail • Dereck Love

This hike takes you through Rock City from ① one end of Rock City Trail to the other end where ② Wall Point Road and Summit Trail meet. During late spring and early summer, you are greeted with brilliant splashes of color from a variety of wildflowers common in the chaparral area.

A few yards to the right of this intersection is the beginning of the rather steep Staircase Trail. The top of this trail joins ③ Summit Trail again, where you can enjoy an expansive view of San Ramon Valley to the west and Rock City immediately below. Head north on Summit Trail, cross South Gate Road, and look for the trail sign to ④ Wildcat Trail, which takes you back across the paved road and down toward Barbecue Terrace Horse and Group Camp. Continue on ⑤ Barbecue Terrace Road through the wide open space that heads down toward Pine Canyon.

At the end of the open space, ⑥ Secret Trail heads off to the left. This begins your mostly shady return trip up the side of Pine Canyon to Pine Ridge. Enjoy an abundance of colorful spring wildflowers on this beautiful, hidden gem of a trail: mariposa lilies, bush monkeyflowers, Indian warriors, deer weed, Ithuriel's spears, and more. Turn left on ⑦ Wall Point Road to return to the intersection of Rock City Trail and Summit Trail. Rather than retracing your steps through Rock City, take Summit Trail to the right, skirting the north side of Rock City. Pass ⑧ Live Oak Campground and follow the paved road past Elephant Rock to Lower Rock City and back to the trailhead.

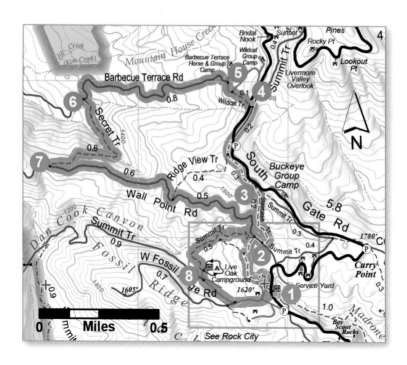

25 Trail Through Time

Distance, difficulty:	6.4 miles one way, strenuous
Cumulative climb:	3,562 feet
Trailhead:	Lower Rock City (J10), or others

"Greenstone" Panel along Juniper Trail • Dereck Love

The rocks of Mount Diablo tell a story of previous landscapes, climates, and life forms as well as epic journeys of tectonic plates. Panels along the Trail Through Time help you read the geologic story written in the rocks as you travel through 190 million years of geologic time. Interspersed with the geologic panels are panels on history, geography, and ecology. A free Trail Through Time brochure, available at the entrance station, will help guide you. To keep you on track, look for the small, octagonal Trail Through Time signs on the trail posts along the way.

Consider traversing the Trail Through Time as two or more separate hikes, each starting and ending at a trailhead easily reached within the park. Rock City is the closest trailhead to the start of the Trail Through Time.

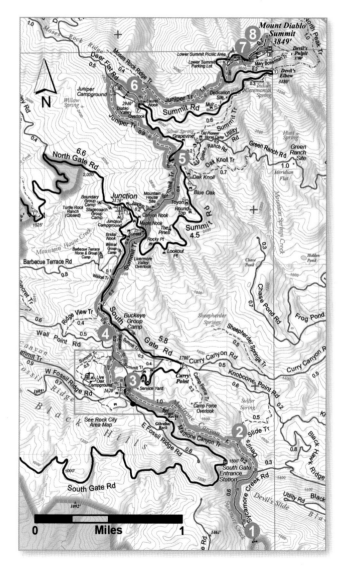

Other suggested starting points are Sunset Picnic Area near the Junction Ranger Station, Diablo Valley Overlook near Juniper Campground, and Lower Summit Picnic Area.

The Trail Through Time begins on ❶ Sycamore Creek Road near the southern park boundary. As you walk north toward the mountain, you journey over 12-million-year-old rocks formed in a shallow sea. Look for shell fossils as you walk. Continue left on Devil's Slide Trail to ❷ Madrone Canyon Trail and up to Rock City. At Rock City, you pass over 50-million-year-old sandstone with unusual erosion features. Cross South Gate Road to follow ❸ Rock City Trail to Summit Trail on the right and up Staircase Trail shortly thereafter on the left. Turn left again back onto ❹ Summit Trail, which crosses South Gate Road and then Summit Road, until you reach ❺ Juniper Trail, partially hidden in the chaparral on the left. Follow Juniper Trail to Juniper Campground and to ❻ Laurel Nook Group Picnic Area. At the far end of the picnic area, Juniper Trail continues up to the Lower Summit Picnic Area. The final section of the Trail Through Time takes you on ❼ Mary Bowerman Trail to ❽ an overlook to the north with a view of Mount Diablo's ocean crust rocks.

Retrace the Trail Through Time path to return to your trailhead, or refer to the Trail Map of Mount Diablo State Park for other interesting, alternate routes back.

Turritella Fossils along Staircase Trail • Mike Woodring

Greenstone along Juniper Trail • Dereck Love

Mary Bowerman Trail Overlook Panel • Dereck Love

26 China Wall and Little Yosemite

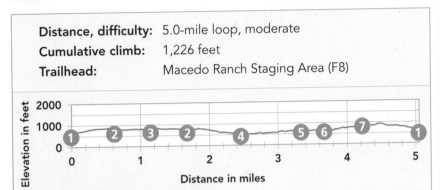

Distance, difficulty:	5.0-mile loop, moderate
Cumulative climb:	1,226 feet
Trailhead:	Macedo Ranch Staging Area (F8)

China Wall • Bill Karieva

The Macedo Ranch area is the site of the park's demonstration ranch, so expect to see cattle during the initial stages of your hike along ❶ Wall Point Road. The picturesque landscape includes undulating hills, scattered groves, and sandstone outcrops. In summer, the grassy pasture becomes a carpet of pale gold.

Veer left onto Briones-Mount Diablo Regional Trail. Take ❷ a 1.1-mile round-trip side excursion down China Wall Road on the left to the strange phenomenon of ❸ "China Wall," a sandstone stratum in an advanced, terminal stage of erosion, tilted into vertical position by the upthrust of Mount Diablo. With adjacent strata eroded away more rapidly, the remnant is, indeed, a wall-like structure, like its man-made equivalent in China. Examine the grotesquely convoluted formations, sculpted by an imaginative Mother Nature. With luck you might spot poorwills nesting in this area.

Now retrace your steps and turn left to begin your descent along ② Little Yosemite Trail into Little Yosemite, a narrow valley with many features of its namesake, Yosemite National Park: imposing cliffs, fantastic rock formations, waterfalls, flower-strewn meadows, all on a much smaller scale.

The path passes through a gate into Diablo Foothills Regional Park. Nearby on your right is another gate to reenter Mount Diablo State Park at Stage Road. ④ Stage Road follows the riparian environment of Pine Creek, with its cool canopy of mature deciduous trees offering glimpses through the foliage of Castle Rock high to the north. Four stream crossings before reaching Pine Pond can present a challenge in wet weather. ⑤ Pine Pond, almost completely silted up, is a haven for numerous bird species. ⑥ Dusty Road lifts you out of Pine Canyon, and ⑦ Wall Point Road takes you back to the trailhead. The meadows along Wall Point Road offer fine flower displays in spring, particularly Ithuriel's spear. At the highest point of Wall Point Road, turn around to enjoy a magnificent view of Mount Diablo, particularly impressive in the mists of late fall and winter.

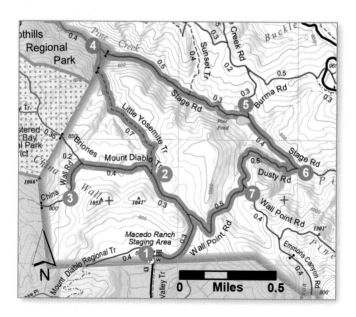

27 Wall Point and Pine Canyon

Distance, difficulty: 7.5-mile loop, strenuous
Cumulative climb: 2,432 feet
Trailhead: Macedo Ranch Staging Area (F8)

California Poppies along Barbecue Terrace Road • Dereck Love

With rolling meadowlands, oak savannas, riparian habitat, great birding, hogbacks, sandstone fantasies, and fine views of the main peak, this pleasant day hike has plenty to recommend it.

The loop follows ❶ Wall Point Road along Pine Ridge, offering striking flower displays in spring, particularly Ithuriel's spear. Turn left onto ❷ Ridge View Trail. The short but steep Ridge View Trail ends at

3 Summit Trail. Turn left and continue on Summit Trail to **4** Wildcat Trail, crossing South Gate Road twice, and take this short trail west and down to **5** Barbecue Terrace Road, which winds through grasslands and descends into Pine Canyon, eventually joining **6** Stage Road. Follow Stage Road to the left. At a trail intersection on the left side of Stage Road, **7** Dusty Road takes you across Pine Ridge back to **8** Wall Point Road. Turn right onto Wall Point Road to return to the trailhead. At the highest point of Wall Point Road, turn around to enjoy a magnificent view of Mount Diablo, particularly impressive in the swirling mists of late fall and winter.

Be aware that roads get muddy in wet weather.

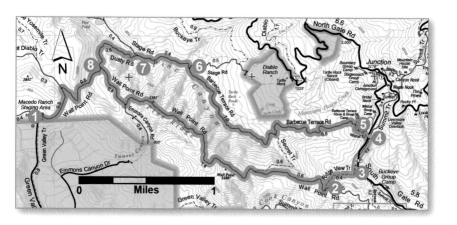

28 Jackass Canyon

Distance, difficulty: 4.5-mile round trip, easy to moderate
Cumulative climb: 801 feet
Trailhead: Finley Road (Q13)

View from Jackass Canyon • Hank Fabian

This hike's destination is a peaceful, grassy meadow surrounded by craggy wilderness above, with few remnants of its colorful history.

The hike begins at the roadside parking area on ① Finley Road three quarters of a mile from the trailhead. Walk beside the road, and use the pedestrian path around a private road gate. Keep left at the junction with ② Old Finley Road, which, at this point, is in a section of Mount Diablo State Park administered by East Bay Regional Park District (EBRPD). Turn left onto ③ Riggs Canyon Road, crossing the boundary of the administered area. Shortly, ④ Jackass Canyon Trail begins and ⑤ ends in less than half a mile in an open meadow.

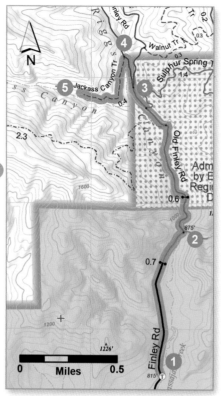

Local residents gave the canyon its name because of its history during the Prohibition years, from 1920 to 1933. Jackass whiskey, allegedly named because it had a bite like a mule and a kick like a horse, was secretly made in this remote canyon. According to the *Mountain Lore* book, "Distilleries or stills were constructed in this canyon bottom because of the abundance of yearlong water from the west fork of Tassajara Creek. The creek was fed by an active spring that the moonshiners tapped by means of piping and a springbox. Armed sentries stood guard at strategic locations above the canyon to be on the lookout for Prohibition agents and robbers."

Distance, difficulty: 7.4-mile round trip, strenuous
Cumulative climb: 2,237 feet
Trailhead: Finley Road (Q13)

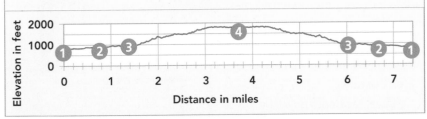

View from Oyster Point Trail • Ruth Ann Kishi

This hike explores some of the least visited parts of the park and offers an unusual opportunity to spot fossils of oysters, for which the point was named.

The hike begins even before entering the park because of the distance from ❶ the parking area on Finley Road to the trailhead.

Walk along the side of the road, and use the pedestrian path around a private road gate. Keep left at the junction with ❷ Old Finley Road. The hike up Old Finley Road to ❸ the beginning of Oyster Point Trail is in a section of Mount Diablo State Park administered by East Bay Regional Park District.

Oyster Point Trail rises gradually along the side of Jackass Canyon before emerging out of the sheltering canopy of oaks and sycamores. Follow this trail until you reach ❹ an informal trail to your left, marked by a trail sign below the summit of Oyster Point. You may wish to explore Oyster Point ridge and its wonderful vistas, but there is no official trail—and lots of poison oak. ❺ The summit is a Miocene sandstone hogback, where you can view the glorious panorama of San Ramon below you and the Bay Area beyond, and, in the opposite direction, the wilderness of Jackass Canyon far below.

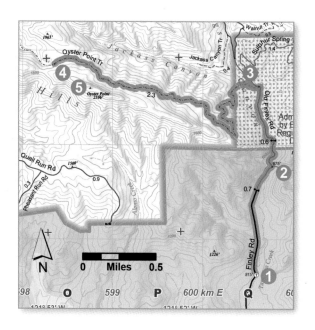

INTERIOR TRAILHEADS

Lower Summit Picnic Area (L6)

Location: On the south side of Summit Road at an elevation of 3,650 feet, just below the Mount Diablo summit.

Parking: Continue through the picnic area to reach a large parking lot.

Facilities: Drinking water, restrooms, park map display, picnic area, visitor center nearby at the summit open daily.

Day use fee: Collected at the South Gate and North Gate entrance stations.

Devil's Elbow (L6)

Location: At the roadside parking area known as Devil's Elbow at an elevation of 3,480 feet, on Summit Road at the last sharp bend just below the Lower Summit Picnic Area.

Parking: Very limited parking off the road. Alternatively, park at Lower Summit parking lot and walk down a short section of Summit Trail.

Facilities: Park map display. Nearest facilities are at the Lower Summit Picnic Area.

Day use fee: Collected at the South Gate and North Gate entrance stations.

Lower Summit Picnic Area • Mike Woodring

⚙ Diablo Valley Overlook (K7)

Location: At the Diablo Valley Overlook roadside parking area at an elevation of 2,940 feet, on Summit Road near the entrance to Juniper Campground. Look for the Juniper Trail signposts near the Laurel Nook Group Picnic Area, where the one-way campground loop road exits Juniper Campground at Summit Road.

Parking: Ample parking on the wide paved pullout.

Facilities: Drinking water, restrooms, campground, picnic area in Juniper Campground.

Day use fee: Collected at the South Gate and North Gate entrance stations.

⚙ Junction Picnic Area (J8)

Location: At the upper end of the Junction Picnic Area loop road, opposite the ranger station at the junction of North Gate and South Gate roads at an elevation of 2,170 feet.

Parking: Very limited parking in the picnic area near the trailhead.

Facilities: Drinking water, restrooms, campground, park map display near the ranger station.

Day use fee: Collected at the South Gate and North Gate entrance stations.

Distance, difficulty: 0.7-mile loop, easy
Cumulative climb: 255 feet
Trailhead: Lower Summit Picnic Area (L6)

Mary Bowerman Trail • Dereck Love

This deservedly popular nature trail is best negotiated with the help of an interpretive trail guide available in the Summit Visitor Center and at the trailhead. The loop hike completely encircles the summit of Mount Diablo, following the contours of the terrain. It is fairly level, with a gentle climb at the end. Incomparable views of the California landscape far below are enhanced by the unusual trailside vegetation, with fine flower displays in spring and early summer. Of primary interest are the various stages of vegetative recovery following the great fire of 1977 on the north and the more recent 2013 fire on the south. Spectacular rock outcrops of ancient Franciscan Complex rocks abound.

Bitterroot along Mary Bowerman Trail • Kevin Hintsa

❶ Mary Bowerman Trail begins at the end of the one-way road on its descent from the Summit. Originally built by the California Conservation Corps, the first third of the trail is accessible and is paved to ❷ the Ransom Point overlook, a good place to spot distant landmarks from comfortable benches. As you continue and turn onto the south side of the mountain, you will see on your left ❸ Devil's Pulpit, a towering red-colored monolith made up of chert. Notice the change in habitat along this side of the mountain as you complete the circle of the summit.

This trail is named to honor celebrated botanist Dr. Mary Leo Bowerman, co-founder of Save Mount Diablo and a charter member of Mount Diablo Interpretive Association.

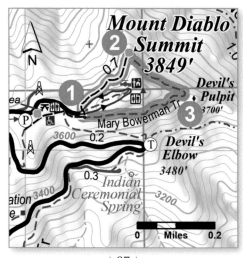

31 Summit Trail and Juniper Trail

Distance, difficulty: 3.8-mile loop, moderate
Cumulative climb: 1,479 feet
Trailhead: Lower Summit Picnic Area (L6)

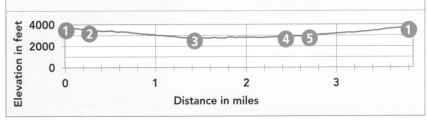

Early Morning View from Summit Trail • Dereck Love

Although it covers a relatively short distance at less than four miles, this rewarding loop hike packs in a variety of features: big views, spring wildflowers, and a lovely section of forest. The hike can begin at various points (Lower Summit Picnic Area, Devil's Elbow, or Juniper Campground), and can be navigated clockwise or counter-clockwise, depending on your preference for elevation gain at the beginning or end of your hike.

From the Lower Summit Picnic Area, descend along ❶ Summit Trail to ❷ Devil's Elbow. From Devil's Elbow, Summit Trail continues below, roughly parallel to the Summit Road. In spring, wildflowers abound along the trail. Enjoy a panoramic view of Curry Canyon far below. The trail descends gradually to the Old Pioneer Horse Camp at Green Ranch Road. Continue along Summit Trail until you reach the paved Summit Road again. A short distance across Summit Road, ❸ Juniper Trail begins. The trail passes through several small, stream-cut shaded valleys, and then opens into a magnificent panoramic view of the southwest slope of Mount Diablo, which includes oak woodland, grassland, riparian, and chaparral communities. Upon reaching ❹ Juniper Campground, follow the loop road to the Laurel Nook Group Picnic Area, where the loop road meets Summit Road. At the far end of the picnic area, ❺ Juniper Trail continues as a nicely graded trail through the dark mixed oak and laurel forest to Moses Rock Ridge. Some steep and rocky sections pass through areas with fire evidence faintly visible from the 1977 fire on the northwest side of the trail and scorched areas still recovering from the 2013 fire on the southeast side. The trail crosses the main Summit Road and ends at the Lower Summit Picnic Area.

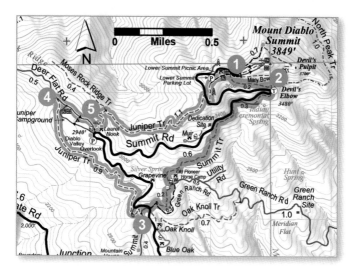

32 The Valentine

Distance, difficulty:	11.2-mile loop, very strenuous
Cumulative climb:	5,671 feet
Trailhead:	Lower Summit Picnic Area (L6)

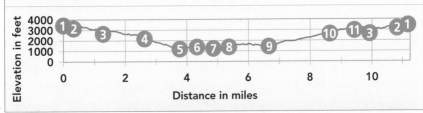

Along Falls Trail • Jack McKeown

This unique hike is an ideal Valentine's Day outing for hike-minded soulmates. Visit the Summit Visitor Center either before or after the hike and enjoy the magnificent—dare we say "romantic"—views from the observation deck. In spring, you and your Valentine will be greeted by the romantic sight of abundant wildflowers along most of the trails.

From ❶ the Lower Summit Picnic Area, it's off to ❷ Devil's Elbow and ❸ Prospectors Gap. From Prospectors Gap, look for Bald Ridge Trail on the left. Marvel at the miniature gardens and the expansive view near Bald Knob. Descend through the manzanitas to Murchio Gap, where a rocky outcrop provides a cozy spot to share a snack. Follow **4** Back Creek Trail down for glimpses of Back Creek, then turn right onto **5** Meridian Point Trail where buttercups, milkmaids, and Indian warriors lurk. Upon reaching **6** Meridian Ridge Road, enjoy a grand vista of Eagle Peak in the distance. Don't miss the right turn onto **7** Middle Trail, partially hidden in the chaparral. Enjoy the fragrant chamise and black sage along Middle Trail to **8** Falls Trail. What can be more romantic than lovely falls and cascades along Falls Trail after winter rains?

Next, take Cardinet Oaks Road a short distance to **9** Olympia Trail, to Mount Olympia Road, then to Zippe Trail and East Trail to ascend **10** Mount Olympia, and record your memorable day in the sign-in log attached to the summit signpost. From Mount Olympia, North Peak Trail leads you to **11** North Peak Road, back to **3** Prospectors Gap and **2** Devil's Elbow again. It's a short distance up Summit Trail to reach the end of this romantic hike. Celebrate with a nice dinner out.

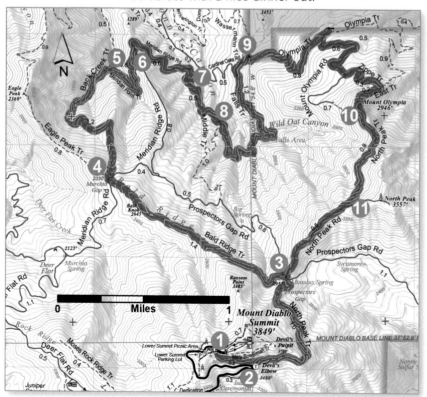

33 Mount Olympia via North Peak Trail

Distance, difficulty: 4.7-mile round trip, moderate to strenuous
Cumulative climb: 2,285 feet
Trailhead: Devil's Elbow (L6)

Approaching Mount Olympia • Dereck Love

This hike is for people who enjoy unlimited sky above and views into distant depths below. Your destination, Mount Olympia, is like a throne, high above the encircling landscape, where you can sit and observe the tiny world below, and beyond, the great plains of the Central Valley. In wintertime, mists roiling up from the depths of Donner Canyon put on a show of landscape hide-and-seek.

The single-track **1** North Peak Trail from Devil's Elbow to Prospectors Gap is a showplace for wildflowers in the spring. From Prospectors Gap, take **2** North Peak Road toward North Peak. Just before the road rises sharply to reach the North Peak summit, veer left onto **3** North Peak Trail toward Mount Olympia. A visitor register is attached to the sign post at **4** the summit of Mount Olympia.

Please note that the descent (and climb back) from North Peak to Mount Olympia is very steep and on slippery scree. Sections of North Peak Trail above Prospectors Gap are also steep and slippery.

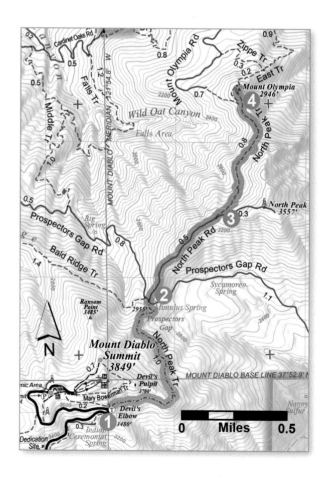

34 Deer Flat Road from Juniper Campground

Distance, difficulty:	1.4-mile round trip, easy
Cumulative climb:	483 feet
Trailhead:	Diablo Valley Overlook (K7)

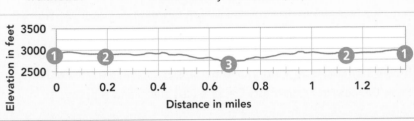

Deer Flat Road • Dereck Love

This pleasant walk highlights fine views into San Ramon Valley across grassy slopes, emerald green in the springtime, with some of the most spectacular California poppy displays on the mountain. The thick grasses thrive in the deep soil of the steep slumps below you, erosion products of the summit rocks. Each season brings new color surprises—the golden grasses against the deep blue sky in summer, and the same grasses, now a silvery gray, bathed in the mists of winter.

This short hike starts at the entrance to Laurel Nook Group Picnic Area and follows ① Juniper Trail to the far end of Juniper Campground to ② Deer Flat Road. Deer Flat Road runs an essentially level course for half a mile to its junction with ③ Burma Road.

Instead of returning by the same path, you might consider an alternate route through Juniper Campground. When you return to the campground, rather than continuing straight, turn right onto the campground road and follow it as it circles back to the parking area (watch for vehicle traffic coming in the opposite direction!). Along the way, enjoy magnificent panoramic views of Diablo Valley and beyond.

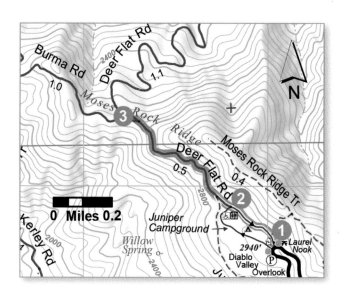

35 Moses Rock Ridge

Distance, difficulty:	1.2-mile round trip, easy
Cumulative climb:	416 feet
Trailhead:	Diablo Valley Overlook (K7)

View from Moses Rock Ridge • Mike Woodring

This hike features some of the most amazing panoramic views on the mountain.

To reach Moses Rock Ridge Trail, take the short section of ① Juniper Trail, which starts its uphill climb at the end of Laurel Nook Group Picnic Area. The climb takes you to a T-junction, where ② Moses Rock Ridge Trail veers to the left. It is ③ a dead-end trail, and the hike thus involves a return trip.

As you climb to the top of the ridge, you will walk along a formation known as a hogback. Hogbacks are formed by strata tilted into vertical position by the upthrust of the main peak and subsequently eroded to leave a platform just a few feet wide, with abrupt drop-offs on each side. Trees and bushes are absent from the ridge top, thus offering unobstructed views of the mountain's surrounding topography and lands far beyond. Some of those views are unmatched: the profile of the entire Eagle Peak massif silhouetted against a Central Valley background; dense forest covering the flanks of the main peak; vigorous junipers, scrub oaks, and gray pines in areas recovered from the devastation of the 1977 fire. Your progress along the gently undulating ridge is enhanced by picturesque formations of almost completely eroded chert, its deep color riddled with milkstone intrusions. In springtime enjoy massive wildflower displays, particularly on the west-facing slopes. Even in late summer, you may find little fiery explosions of California fuchsias struggling to survive in their cherty environment.

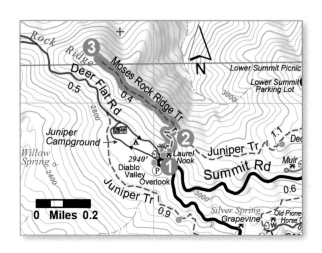

36 Juniper Trail to the Summit

Distance, difficulty: 2.7-mile round trip, easy to moderate
Cumulative climb: 1,023 feet
Trailhead: Diablo Valley Overlook (K7)

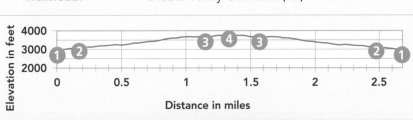

Juniper Trail • Dereck Love

Campers and other visitors at Juniper Campground can explore new terrain, enjoy panoramic vistas, and visit the Summit Visitor Center, all on the same relatively easy hike.

The first part of ❶ Juniper Trail above Laurel Nook Picnic Area is a nicely graded, intimate trail built by the Youth Conservation Corps just before the 1977 fire. Switchbacks (avoid slippery shortcuts) facilitate the climb through the dark mixed oak and laurel forest, survivor of many fires, to ② Moses Rock Ridge. Bear right through vigorous chaparral (beware of possible poison oak next to the trail) to reach several

Bay Laurel Trees near Juniper Campground Area
• Dereck Love

interesting rock outcrops supporting a variety of stunted, tundra-like plants. Some steep and rocky sections pass through areas burned in 1977 and 2013, with fire evidence faintly visible from the 1977 fire on the northwest side of the trail, and scorched areas still recovering from the 2013 fire on the southeast side. The trail crosses Summit Road and ends at ③ the Lower Summit Picnic Area. It's just a short climb up Summit Trail between the one-way roads to reach ④ Mount Diablo's summit. The summit itself is inside the Summit Visitor Center rotunda.

The return trip is all downhill.

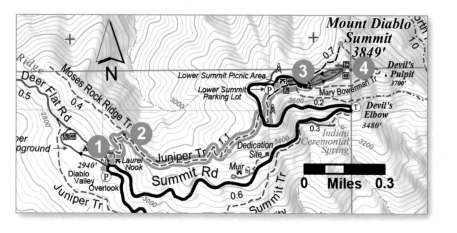

37 Eagle Peak from Juniper Campground

Distance, difficulty:	6.6-mile round trip, moderate to strenuous
Cumulative climb:	2,582 feet
Trailhead:	Diablo Valley Overlook (K7)

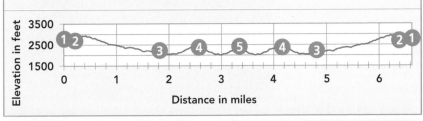

Eagle Peak • Mike Woodring

This hike features an invigorating variety of environments and challenges.

Begin your hike at the entrance to Laurel Nook Group Picnic Area and follow ① Juniper Trail to the far end of Juniper Campground to ② Deer Flat Road. On your way down Deer Flat Road to Deer Flat, one of the mountain's most memorable beauty spots, you will enjoy flower-strewn meadows in spring. Once in Deer Flat, you will be treated to a symphony of bird songs. Bear right onto ③ Meridian Ridge Road, down to the Deer Flat Creek crossing, and then up to Murchio Gap, where ④ Eagle Peak Trail begins on the left. Eagle Peak Trail is an exhilarating "hogback," a long, crested ridge, often only a few feet wide, with sharp drop-offs on either side. At an elevation of 2,369 feet, ⑤ Eagle Peak provides a stunning view of the expanse of Contra Costa's Central Valley, and a great place to pause for a break on several rocks nature has conveniently placed for this purpose.

Retrace your steps back to the trailhead.

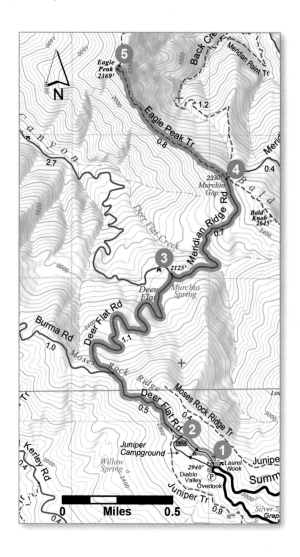

38 Grand Loop

Distance, difficulty:	6.3-mile loop, strenuous
Cumulative climb:	2,521 feet
Trailhead:	Diablo Valley Overlook (K7)

Eagle Peak from Deer Flat Road • Dereck Love

On this clockwise circumambulation of the mountain's summit, you will discover some of the park's most attractive hidden trails. With its profusion of bird song, Deer Flat is a restful place for a quick break. Bald Ridge Trail features a new surprise every few yards: a tiny rock garden, an unexpected vista, perhaps a sighting of an elusive California thrasher before it scurries into the dense shrubs rather than flying away. North

Peak Trail offers fantastic displays of wildflowers in the spring, including the rarely seen wind poppies. Juniper Trail has its own set of rock gardens featuring tundra-like stunted plants.

Start your hike at Laurel Nook Group Picnic Area and follow ❶ Juniper Trail to the far end of Juniper Campground to Deer Flat Road and down to Deer Flat. For the complete loop, take right turns at each junction: ❷ Meridian Ridge Road to Murchio Gap; ❸ Bald Ridge Trail to Prospectors Gap; ❹ North Peak Trail to Devil's Elbow; ❺ Summit Trail to the Lower Summit Picnic Area; and ❻ Juniper Trail back down to Juniper Campground and the trailhead.

Circumnavigating Mount Diablo's summit from the Lower Summit Picnic Area (L6) in the opposite (counterclockwise) direction is another popular option for making a "grand loop." Upon completing the loop, treat yourself to an ice cream bar at the Summit Visitor Center!

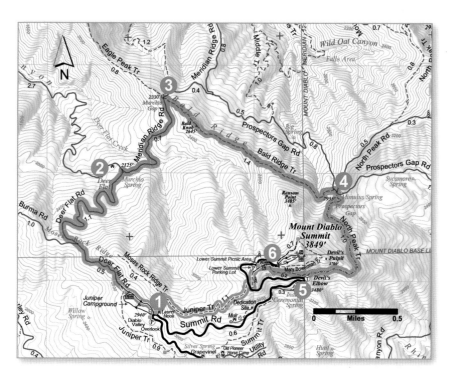

Distance, difficulty:	0.5-mile round trip, easy
Cumulative climb:	213 feet
Trailhead:	Junction Picnic Area (J8)

Site of Mountain House • Mike Woodring

Mountain House was a resort and weekend goal for Bay Area residents over 100 years ago.

The steadily climbing ❶ Junction Trail follows the old stage coach road that went to Mountain House. This trail joins Summit Trail after

0.2 miles. ② The former hotel site is about 200 yards beyond on Summit Trail.

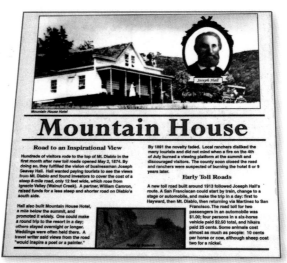

Mountain House Hotel

Mountain House

Road to an Inspirational View

Hundreds of visitors rode to the top of Mt. Diablo in the first month after new toll roads opened May 2, 1874. By doing so, they fulfilled the vision of businessman Joseph Seavey Hall. Hall wanted paying tourists to see the views from Mt. Diablo and found investors to cover the cost of a steep 8-mile road, only 12 feet wide, which rose from Ignacio Valley (Walnut Creek). A partner, William Camron, raised funds for a less steep and shorter road on Diablo's south side.

Hall also built Mountain House Hotel, a mile below the summit, and promoted it widely. One could make a round trip to the resort in a day; others stayed overnight or longer. Weddings were often held there. A travel writer said views from the road "would inspire a poet or a painter."

By 1891 the novelty faded. Local ranchers disliked the many tourists and did not mind when a fire on the 4th of July burned a viewing platform at the summit and discouraged visitors. The county soon closed the road and ranchers were suspected of burning the hotel 8 or 9 years later.

Early Toll Roads

A new toll road built around 1913 followed Joseph Hall's route. A San Franciscan could start by train, change to a stage or automobile, and make the trip in a day: first to Hayward, then Mt. Diablo, then returning via Martinez to San Francisco. The road toll for two passengers in an automobile was $1.00; four persons in a six-horse vehicle paid $2.50 total, and hikers paid 25 cents. Some animals cost almost as much as people: 10 cents per horse or cow, although sheep cost two for a nickel.

Joseph Hall

Interpretive Panel at Mountain House Site
• Mike Woodring

As you climb toward the site, distant views of the coastal ranges slowly vanish, and you enter an imposing bowl-like enclosure in the heart of the mountain encircled by grassy cliffs and forest. No trace is left of the old hotel. Interpretive signs at the site help us envision the excitement that the arrival of the stage coach must have engendered a century ago.

Return via the same route.

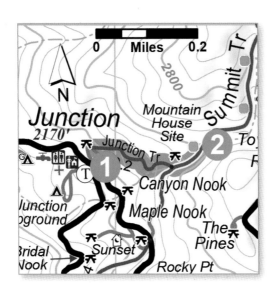

Camel Rock Trail • Carl Nielson

North Gate Road Park Boundary (F6)

Location: On North Gate Road a little over a mile beyond the entrance station near the brown park boundary sign (F6).

Parking: A pull-off at the side of the road accommodates several vehicles.

Facilities: Park map display. Nearest facilities are at the Junction Ranger Station.

Day use fee: Collected at the North Gate entrance station.

 Burma Road (H7)

Location: The Burma Road intersection with North Gate Road at an elevation of 963 feet.

Parking: Very limited parking at the roadside.

Facilities: No facilities. Nearest facilities are at the Junction Ranger Station.

Day use fee: Collected at the North Gate entrance station.

Diablo Ranch (I8)

Location: The parking pullout across from Diablo Ranch on North Gate Road.

Parking: Limited parking at the gravel pullout.

Facilities: No facilities. Nearest facilities are at the Junction Ranger Station.

Day use fee: Collected at the North Gate entrance station.

40 Camel Rock Trail

Distance, difficulty: 3.1-mile loop, easy to moderate
Cumulative climb: 975 feet
Trailhead: On North Gate Road Park Boundary (F6)

Camel Rock • Kevin Hintsa

From the lowest reaches of the mountain, not often visited, formations of severely eroded greenstone are seen at the sides of Camel Rock Trail as it ascends through alternating zones of grasslands, chaparral, and oak savannas. Several small streams cross the path, with tiny waterfalls highlighting an intimate riparian environment even in the heat of summer. The trail crosses rolling grasslands completely devoid of shrubs and trees, a band of serpentinic soil with outcrops of slick green serpentine and, in good years, an astounding display of springtime California poppies.

Look on the north side of North Gate Road for ❶ the narrow Camel Rock Trail climbing steeply to the right. At the high point of the loop as you approach North Gate Road, take a slight detour for a glimpse of ❷ Camel Rock, the namesake of the trail. Walk up Burma Road to the point where the road begins to rise steeply, cross the meadow to your right, and the rock soon pops into view. Retrace your steps, head down Burma Road, and cross North Gate Road. Continue on Burma Road to ❸ Little Pine Creek Road, which takes you back to the trailhead.

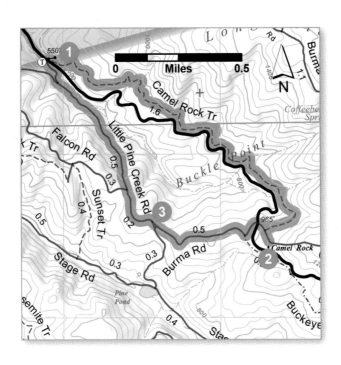

41 Castle Rock Trail

Distance, difficulty: 3.1-mile loop, easy to moderate
Cumulative climb: 858 feet
Trailhead: On North Gate Road Park Boundary (F6)

View from Castle Rock Trail • Jack McKeown

Castle Rock Trail is the highlight of this loop, an exciting traverse of the narrow ridge formed by the spectacular rock formations of Pine Canyon. With luck, you may spot the swift flight of peregrine falcons.

From the North Gate Road park boundary, follow ❶ Little Pine Creek Road as it descends a short distance to the creek, cross it, and take a sharp right onto ❷ Falcon Road. Follow Falcon Road to its junction with ❸ Castle Rock Trail, which starts as a wide road on the right, but soon changes to a single-track trail. Continue on Castle Rock Trail to ❹ Castle Rock itself. Retrace your steps back to Falcon Road and turn right onto Falcon Road to eventually meet Little Pine Creek Road. A left turn onto ❺ Little Pine Creek Road completes the loop back to the trailhead. Falcon and Little Pine Creek roads offer an abundance of surprises: shaded mature oak woodlands, an unexpected year-round pond that provides a welcome wildlife refuge, and broad yellow swatches of aromatic tarweed in fall. Look for the droll tree trunk sculpture on your left as you climb one of the Falcon Road slopes.

Castle Rock Trail is closed to the public during the peregrine falcon nesting season in springtime. Plan on taking this hike during fall or winter. Summer can be hot at the ridge top. This hike is easy except for three rather steep climbs, all quite short.

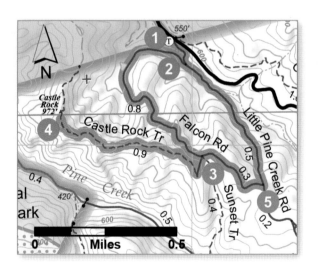

42 Buckeye Trail

Distance, difficulty:	3.4-mile loop, easy to moderate
Cumulative climb:	916 feet
Trailhead:	Burma Road (H7)

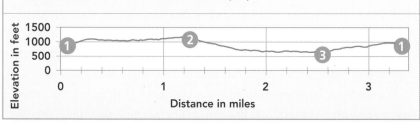

Buckeyes along Buckeye Trail • Mike Woodring

Buckeye Trail gently and gradually descends away from North Gate Road while offering a spectacular view of Pine Canyon and Pine Ridge beyond.

From North Gate Road, it's a short walk down Burma Road to the beginning of ❶ Buckeye Trail on the left. Look for deer grazing near the trail or resting under nearby oak trees. Note the stands of buckeye as you approach Stage Road and the privately held Diablo Ranch. Buckeye Trail is one of the few single-track trails on which bikes are allowed, although cyclists must yield to hikers and horses.

Turn right onto  ② Stage Road. The increasingly steep descent on Stage Road takes you into Pine Canyon. Stage Road follows the riparian environment of Pine Creek, with its cool canopy of mature deciduous trees, until finally

Buckeyes • Mike Woodring

reaching ❸ Pine Pond, which is almost completely silted up and is a haven for numerous bird species.

At Pine Pond, look up to the north and see Burma Road rising to the ridge, challenging you to your final ascent up Burma Road and back to the trailhead.

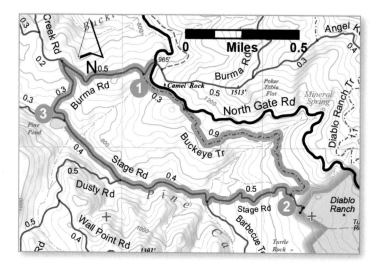

43 Burma Road

Distance, difficulty:	4.1-mile loop, moderate
Cumulative climb:	1,702 feet
Trailhead:	Burma Road (H7)

Long Ridge from Burma Road • Bill Karieva

This loop hike offers excellent bird watching, interesting geology, and a scenic spot to sit and enjoy the views.

Begin by following ① Burma Road east from North Gate Road. After a short but astoundingly steep climb, Burma Road (named for the World War II mountainous supply route) intersects with ② Angel Kerley Road. Continue to the left on Burma Road, past ③ the intersection with Government Road on the left. According to the *Mountain Lore* book,

Government Road was named after Government Ranch, a 3,000-acre ranch on the western slope of Mount Diablo purchased by two U.S. Army officers in 1851.

Burma Road gradually traverses Long Ridge and crosses a broad band of serpentinite and peridotite with its weird rocks and stunted plants, a wildly barren stretch that contrasts with the lush grasses on the undulating slopes. This is a great birding area: rough-legged hawks, ash-throated flycatchers, horned larks. ④ Moses Rock offers a peaceful and scenic rest spot. Beyond the rock and spring, at the point where Burma Road turns sharply upward to the north, look for the beginning of Mother's Trail on the right. Descend on ⑤ Mother's Trail (some sections are very steep!), which ends at ⑥ Angel Kerley Road. Angel Kerley owned and operated Diablo Ranch on North Gate Road. She named Mother's Trail to honor her mother. Turn right onto Angel Kerley Road. This path shortly joins Burma Road again, which takes you back to the trailhead.

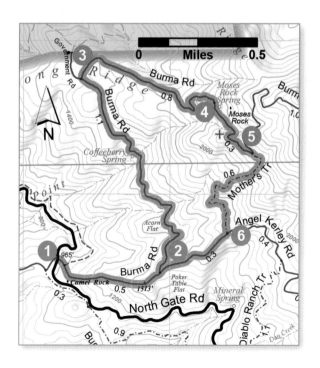

44 Diablo Ranch Trail and Burma Road

Distance, difficulty: 6.1-mile loop, moderate to strenuous
Cumulative climb: 2,440 feet
Trailhead: Diablo Ranch (I8)

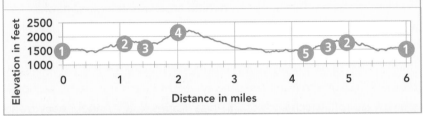

Mountain Goldfish near Burma Road • Mike Woodring

This six-mile hike climbs up some of the steepest trails on the mountain. Follow ❶ Diablo Ranch Trail to its intersection with Angel Kerley Road, passing through grassy fields dotted with wildflowers in the spring, and fragrant California bay laurel and chaparral the rest of the year. To your left are panoramic views of San Ramon's Las Trampas, Pleasanton Ridge, and the north side of the mountain, studded with stately oaks, massive rock formations, and Diablo Ranch itself, still privately owned.

A left turn onto ❷ Angel Kerley Road takes you to Mother's Trail. When you reach ❸ Mother's Trail, turn right and begin the steep climb. On clear days, you will be rewarded with a view of the summit of Mount Diablo. Looking down toward North Gate Road, you can see Camel Rock. At the intersection with Burma Road, pause at the water trough and enjoy the unexpected but delightful "mountain" goldfish.

Continue down ❹ Burma Road to the left, passing Moses Rock on your right, through red rocks, Coulter pines, black sage, and more stunning vistas. You may even spot a prairie falcon. Notice the coarsely crystalline pyroxenite exposed along Burma Road and sparkling in the sunlight. Return to ❺ Angel Kerley Road and turn left, retracing your steps when you reach Diablo Ranch Trail, back to the starting point.

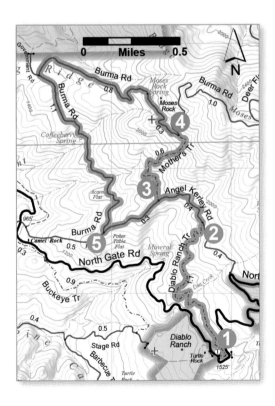

Oak Hills Trail to Perkins Canyon • Mike Woodring

Sharkey Road (N3)

Location: On Marsh Creek Road, about one and a half miles east of Regency Drive in the town of Clayton. Sharkey Road begins beyond a locked gate; pass through a gap on its right.

Parking: Limited parking at a wide pull-off with a prominent blue cell box on a pole on the south side of Marsh Creek Road. Do not block access.

Facilities: No facilities.

Day use fee: Not collected.

✺ Three Springs Road (N3)

Location: On Marsh Creek Road, about two miles east of Regency Drive in the town of Clayton, you will pass under power lines. Just beyond, Three Springs Road is the gated road on the right side of Marsh Creek Road.

Parking: Limited parking on the wide shoulder of Marsh Creek Road. Do not block the gate.

Facilities: No facilities.

Day use fee: Not collected.

✺ Morgan Territory Road (O4)

Location: On Morgan Territory Road near Marsh Creek Road. Drive east on Marsh Creek Road from Clayton to its junction with Morgan Territory Road. Turn right onto Morgan Territory Road. After a tenth of a mile, turn into the road entrance on the right with an extensive gravel parking area (shown as P on the trail map).

Parking: Ample parking in the gravel area.

Facilities: No facilities.

Day use fee: Not collected.

✺ Red Corral (R10)

Location: On Morgan Territory Road heading toward Livermore, about 4.5 miles from Marsh Creek Road junction, 0.4 miles beyond the two narrow one-lane bridges. Red Corral is on the left side of the road, and the state park boundary gate and trailhead are on the right side.

Parking: Very limited roadside parking. Do not block the adjacent road gate that is used by private landowners.

Facilities: No facilities.

Day use fee: Not collected.

45 Three Springs from Sharkey Road

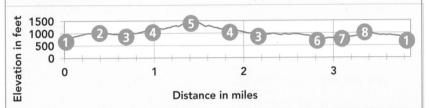

Distance, difficulty: 3.9-mile loop, moderate
Cumulative climb: 1,367 feet
Trailhead: Sharkey Road (N3)

Three Springs Road • Mike Woodring

This hike features an exploration of the Three Springs property acquired by Save Mount Diablo and dedicated to the park in 1993. The moment you step past the trailhead gate, you feel the magic of this exceptional environment: blue oak groves, which gradually reveal the overpowering steep slopes of Mount Olympia directly in front of you.

1 Sharkey Road eventually meets the paved Three Springs Road. Cross this road, and straight ahead find **2** the narrow single-track Sattler Trail, which may be a little faint initially. Sattler Trail is the jewel of this hike, as it plunges into some of the densest forests in the park, dark and mysterious, with seasonal small streams breaking the silence. Sheltered here are magnificent examples of valley oak, unique giants that must be centuries old. If you wish to climb to the springs, turn right onto **3** Quicksilver Trail, then left onto the dead-end **4** Ridgeline Trail. **5** The three active springs are used by private property owners nearby. Please respect their water rights and privacy.

Retrace your steps to **3** Sattler Trail, turn right, and continue until the sharp descent to meet **6** Olympia Trail. Turn left on Olympia Trail to **7** Miwok Road, a gravel fire road. Cross Dunn Creek and follow Miwok Road up to Three Springs Road. Turn right and see **8** Marsh Trail on the left. Marsh Trail leads you to Sharkey Road and your return to the trailhead.

The loop has a few rough single-track stretches. Poison oak is abundant, so long sleeves and pants are recommended.

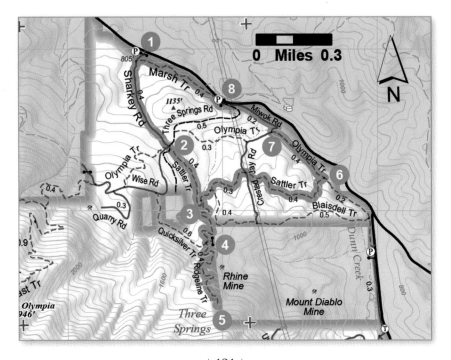

46 Mount Olympia from Three Springs

Distance, difficulty:	5.8-mile round trip, strenuous
Cumulative climb:	2,570 feet
Trailhead:	Three Springs Road (N3)

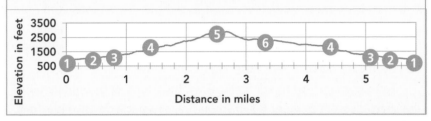

Mount Olympia • Ruth Ann Kishi

Many things attract your attention on this hike: wildflowers well into summer, grotesquely eroded rock formations reminiscent of the American Southwest, the sequence of gradually expanding views. The climax view, of course, is from the Mount Olympia summit itself. This hike covers some of the steepest trails in the park, especially as you reach the flanks of Mount Olympia; bring your trekking poles.

Enter by the gate and walk along the paved ① Three Springs Road as it veers to the right and descends into meadows beyond. Watch for Olympia Trail on your left, which follows the paved road for a short distance. Keep following the Olympia Trail signs. ② The single-track Olympia Trail soon turns away from the paved road to the right and later intersects with Wise Road near the base of Mount Olympia. Turn right onto ③ Wise Road/Olympia Trail, and continue up Olympia Trail until it meets East Trail on the flanks of the mountain. Turn left onto ④ East Trail. At its intersection with Mount Olympia Road, you have just a short distance to go to reach ⑤ the summit of Mount Olympia. A visitor register is maintained at the summit. Descend from the summit and head west via Mount Olympia Road. Turn right onto ⑥ Olympia Trail to return to Three Springs Road and back to Marsh Creek Road.

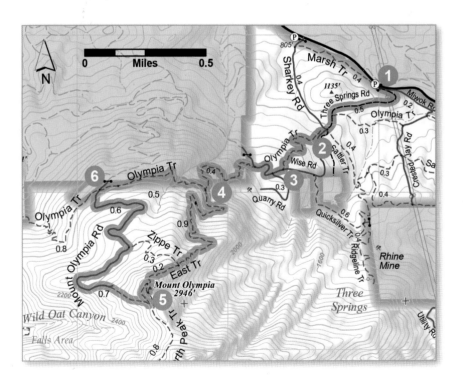

47 Perkins Canyon

Distance, difficulty: 2.6-mile loop, easy
Cumulative climb: 585 feet
Trailhead: Morgan Territory Road (O4)

Perkins Canyon • Hank Fabian

This is an exploration of a quiet and isolated corner of the park, featuring the delightful Perkins Canyon gorge, the imposing vertical cliffs of North Peak, volcanic andesite plugs, and a riot of wildflowers in spring. Look for several stands of the near-endemic Mount Diablo globe lily.

① Oak Hills Trail begins at the fence opening at the south end of the gravel parking area. The trail crosses Dunn Creek (you'll get your boots wet after wet weather). Notice the view of the abandoned mercury mines to the west. Keep right on ➋ Diablo Mines Trail. After gaining some elevation, it veers to the left as ➌ a single-track trail. Notice the flat areas under the valley oak trees where a rural trailer park was located a few decades ago before the land was sold to Mount Diablo State Park. Diablo Mines Trail ends at ➍ the wide Perkins Trail. Turn right, crossing minor streams and the larger Perkins Creek, which is dry in summer, but flows swiftly in winter. Downstream about 100 yards and still standing, but not visible from the trail, are two

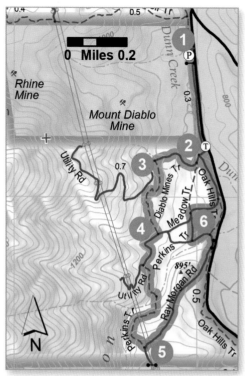

historic dams built for irrigation purposes in the 1920s and 1930s by landowner A.E. Howard, a wealthy Oakland businessman and gentleman horse breeder. The trail climbs to ➎ Ray Morgan Road. Follow this road to the left and to its leftward swing at the end of a long descent, again to meet ➏ Perkins Trail. Turn right and take Perkins Trail back to Oak Hills Trail and the trailhead. This loop may be somewhat challenging due to seasonal stream crossings, abundant poison oak, and some rough trail sections.

The fire of 2013 originated in this area before spreading to the slopes of North Peak and Mount Diablo. Scientists and naturalists will be studying the effects of the fire and recovery here for several years.

Distance, difficulty: 4.3-mile loop, moderate
Cumulative climb: 1,448 feet
Trailhead: Red Corral (R10)

Native American Grinding Holes • Dereck Love

The Amphitheater is a unique phenomenon in the state park, a large bowl formed by embracing cliffs and rocks, a level area of deep soil supporting a growth of lush grasses and magnificent centuries-old oak trees, scattered like giant sentinels across the landscape. The magic of this secret spot is enhanced by its isolation in the far eastern reaches of the park bordering Morgan Territory Road. The abundance of grinding holes near sources of water indicates that Native Americans inhabited this beautiful, bountiful location.

Begin the hike from the park gate across from Red Corral and proceed straight ahead on ❶ Morgan Creek Road. Turn right onto ❷ Jeremiah Creek Trail, left onto ❸ Old Finley Road, and left onto ❹ Amphitheater Trail.

After visiting the Amphitheater, you may retrace your steps for an easy return to the trailhead, or complete the loop as follows, with one rather steep and strenuous climb: left onto ❺ Crestview Road, and left onto ❻ Highland Ridge Road, right onto ❼ Morgan Creek Road and back to Red Corral. You will be rewarded with spectacular views of Mount Diablo in profile and the distant delta region.

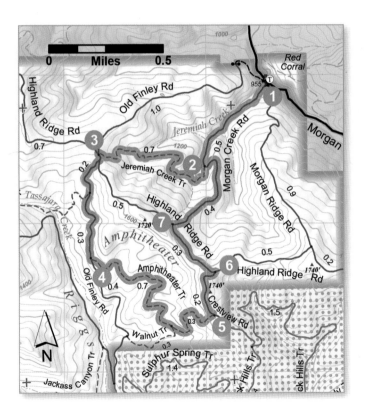

Distance, difficulty: 5.6-mile loop, moderate to strenuous
Cumulative climb: 1,898 feet
Trailhead: Red Corral (R10)

Bob's Pond • Paul Salemme

A highlight of this hike is descending into the dark and mysterious forest sheltering Tassajara Creek and spotting a profusion of forest flowers—in early spring, giant trillium and checker lilies.

After passing through the park gate across from Red Corral, continue straight ahead and upward on ❶ Morgan Creek Road. The steadily rising road parallels Jeremiah Creek in a dense deciduous forest. At a sharp bend, look for a post to your right announcing the start of ② Jeremiah Creek Trail. This delightful narrow path meanders through the unspoiled wilderness of an oak savanna and trailside creek. It rises gently up to the crest of Highland Ridge. ③ Highland Ridge Road is straight ahead. Follow the steep road up to the park boundary. A post on your left marks the beginning of ④ Tassajara Creek Trail. Ahead are broad rolling meadows with orange splashes of poppies, and an unexpected picnic table at the overlook of ⑤ Bob's Pond, a wildlife refuge. The shady trail follows the contours of Tassajara Creek and ends after a steep rise to meet ⑥ Old Finley Road. A left and a short climb take you back to the end of Jeremiah Creek Trail to retrace your steps to Red Corral.

A word of caution: There are patches of trailside poison oak on Jeremiah Creek Trail. Stretches of Tassajara Creek Trail may have been churned up by horses and wild pigs.

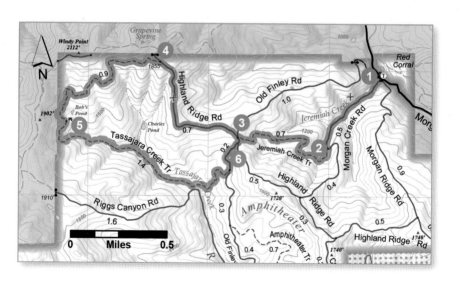

50 Mount Diablo Marathon

Distance:	26 miles, 385 yards
Cumulative climb:	9,666 feet
Trailhead:	Mitchell Canyon Staging Area (J2)

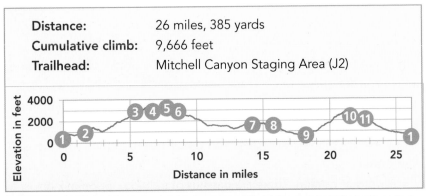

View from Northwest: Mount Diablo Peaks • Stephen Joseph

Some visitors view the park as a place to test their physical and mental endurance. This marathon-length hike should be attempted only by the most physically fit individuals. Late spring is a good time for this hike because daylight hours are longer and wildflowers are in bloom. Start early in the morning and carry a park trails map so you can alter your course should the need arise. Ideally, people who attempt this hike are already familiar with the trails from previous hikes in the park.

The following marathon hike description starts at the Mitchell Canyon Staging Area at the north entrance to the park, near the town of Clayton. However, the hike may be started from other trailheads in the park instead, including Curry Point, Rock City, Devil's Elbow, and Burma Road where it crosses North Gate Road.

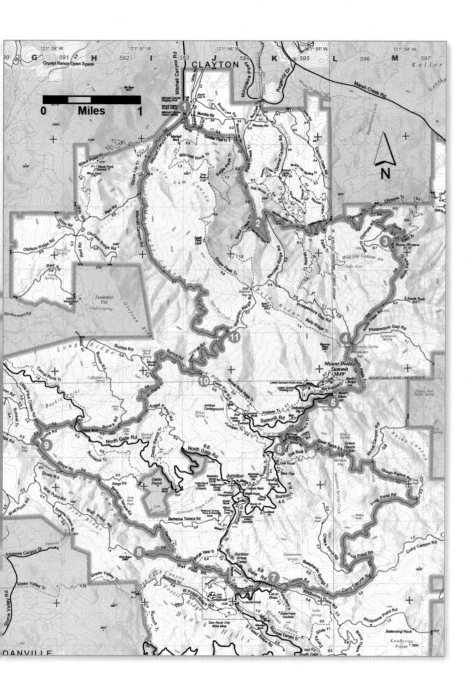

Start from ① Mitchell Canyon Road and make these turns: left onto Oak Road (where the split rail fencing ends), right to Coulter Pine Trail, right to Bruce Lee Road, right to Back Creek Trail, left to ② Meridian Point Trail, left to Meridian Ridge Road, right to Cardinet Oaks Road, right to Olympia Trail, right to Mount Olympia Road, left to Zippe Trail, right to East Trail, left to Mount Olympia Road. Stop to catch your breath at ③ Mount Olympia and enjoy the magnificent view.

View of Wild Oat Canyon
from Mount Olympia • Dereck Love

Next, head south on North Peak Trail, right on North Peak Road, and at Prospectors Gap, continue straight on ④ North Peak Trail. At Devil's Elbow, turn left to ⑤ Summit Trail, left to ⑥ Green Ranch Road, right to Frog Pond Road, and right to Curry Canyon Road. Cross the Curry Point parking lot. ⑦ Camp Force Trail continues along the shoulder of South Gate Road for a short distance to a marked crosswalk. Cross the road and, at the next intersection, turn left to Summit Trail and continue down to South Gate Road. Make the following turns: right up Summit Trail, straight on Wall Point Road, right to ⑧ Secret Trail, left to Barbecue Terrace Road, left to Stage Road, right to ⑨ Burma Road, right to Angel Kerley Road, left to Mother's Trail, right to Burma Road, left to ⑩ Deer Flat Road, and left to ⑪ Mitchell Canyon Road. Return to the Mitchell Canyon trailhead.

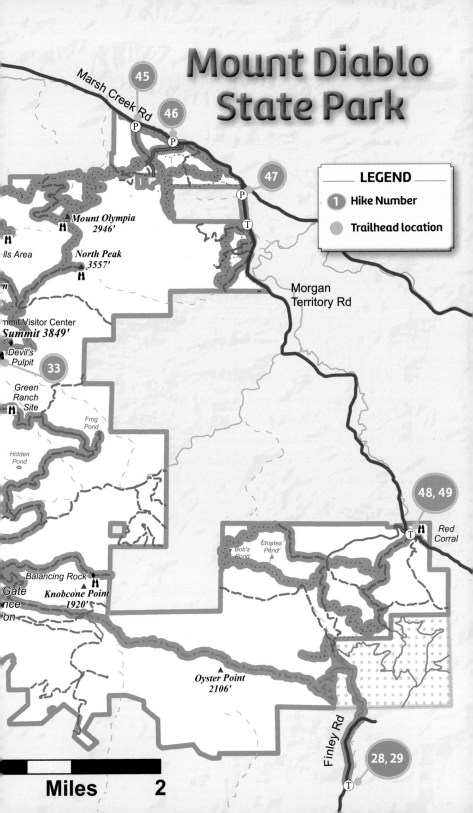

Mount Diablo State Park

Marsh Creek Rd

LEGEND

① Hike Number

⬤ Trailhead location

Mount Olympia
2946'

North Peak
3557'

Morgan
Territory Rd

mmit Visitor Center
Summit 3849'

Devil's
Pulpit

Green
Ranch
Site

Frog
Pond

Hidden
Pond

Bob's
Pond

Charles
Pond

Red
Corral

Balancing Rock
Knobcone Point
1920'

Gate
nce
ion

Oyster Point
2106'

Finley Rd

Miles 2

45 46 47 33 48, 49 28, 29

Ils Area

n

Acknowledgments

This guide book is the culmination of countless miles of hiking in Mount Diablo State Park by many dedicated volunteers of the Mount Diablo Interpretive Association (MDIA). It is an expansion of the three hike brochures for which Frank Valle-Riestra wrote the text in 2001: Short, Pleasant Walks in Mt. Diablo State Park, Moderate Hikes in Mt. Diablo State Park, and Demanding Hikes in Mt. Diablo State Park.

In 2009, a small committee of MDIA members wanted to share their love of hiking in the park and began thinking about their favorite hikes and contributing descriptions of those hikes for this guide. The committee consisted of Leslie Contreras, Helene Cahill, Ruth Ann Kishi, Rich McDrew, Edith Valle-Riestra, Frank Valle-Riestra, and Mike Woodring.

Early on, they compiled a binder with hike descriptions, maps, and profiles of some of the most popular hikes originating from the Mitchell Canyon trailhead and left the binder at the Mitchell Canyon Visitor Center. Who better to provide feedback on the hike data than the docents who offer guidance to hikers coming into the park? For this valuable feedback, we thank the dozens of docents who already have an intimate knowledge of the trails and features in the park.

Our heartfelt thanks go to the following volunteers who contributed their expertise to create this guide book for all to enjoy:

- **Hike descriptions:** Jim Bily, Helene Cahill, Ruth Ann Kishi, Rich McDrew, Debbie McKeown, Edith Valle-Riestra, Frank Valle-Riestra, and Mike Woodring.

- **Maps and profiles:** Daniel Clarke and Mike Woodring. Many other volunteers assisted with gathering accurate trail mileage data, wheeling and rewheeling the trails.

- **Editing and proofreading:** Jim Bily, Leslie Contreras, Sue Donecker, Ruth Ann Kishi, Debbie McKeown, Jerry Schweickert, Edith Valle-Riestra, Frank Valle-Riestra, and Mike Woodring.

- **Photographers:** Joyce Chin, Hank Fabian, Kevin Hintsa, Stephen Joseph, Bill Karieva, Ruth Ann Kishi, Dereck Love, Debbie McKeown, Jack McKeown, Ray Mengel, Carl Nielson, Roi Peers, Paul Salemme, and Mike Woodring.

This publication would not have been possible without the support of Mount Diablo State Park and other California State Parks staff. We thank you for taking your precious time to provide insightful feedback and encouragement.

Mount Diablo Interpretive Association
June 2015

Mount Diablo Interpretive Association

Founded in 1974, the Mount Diablo Interpretive Association (MDIA) promotes public awareness of the natural and cultural history and significance of Mount Diablo through educational programs, events, publications, and outreach. As a nonprofit, all-volunteer cooperative association in partnership with California Department of Parks and Recreation, MDIA helps interpret Mount Diablo State Park for the benefit of the public to enrich visitors' experience in the park. In line with the state's mission, MDIA serves to preserve Mount Diablo's extraordinary beauty and biological diversity, protect its most valued natural and cultural resources, and create opportunities for high-quality outdoor recreation.

MDIA provides assistance to park visitors by providing support for docents at the Summit Visitor Center and the Mitchell Canyon Visitor Center and roving docents out on the trails. MDIA's diverse offerings include educational programs; interpretive books, hiking brochures, and maps; and trails and trail signage development and maintenance, all in support of the extensive work performed by local Mount Diablo State Park staff.

Because MDIA is an all-volunteer organization, almost all net proceeds from sales of merchandise at the visitor centers and via the MDIA website, as well as donations, go directly to the support of Mount Diablo State Park.

Our volunteers thank you for purchasing this guide.

Mount Diablo Interpretive Association
P.O. Box 346, Walnut Creek, CA 94597
925-927-7222 • www.mdia.org

California State Parks Mission

The mission of the California Department of Parks and Recreation is to provide for the health, inspiration, and education of the people of California by helping to preserve the state's extraordinary biological diversity, protecting its most valued natural and cultural resources, and creating opportunities for high-quality outdoor recreation.

California State Parks supports equal access. Prior to arrival at Mount Diablo State Park, visitors with disabilities who need assistance should contact Mount Diablo State Park, (925) 673-2891 (Contra Solano Sector Office of the Bay Area District), or (925) 837-6129 (Junction Ranger Station).

This publication, *Hiker's Guide to Mount Diablo State Park*, is available in alternate formats by contacting Mount Diablo State Park, (925) 673-2891.

- California State Parks
  P.O. Box 942896
  Sacramento, CA 94296-0001
  Telephone: (800) 777-0369

- Outside the U.S.: International Calling Code + (916) 653-6995

- TTY Relay Service: 711

- www.parks.ca.gov

- Mount Diablo State Park
  96 Mitchell Canyon Road
  Clayton, CA 94517-1500
  (925) 837-2525 (General Information)

Index

ε C

D

E

&F

&G

H

I

J

&K

&L

&M

❧T

ॐ U

ॐ V

ॐ W,X,Y,Z